The Soul of
Classical American Philosophy

D1565260

The Soul of
Classical American Philosophy

*The Ethical and Spiritual Insights of William James,
Josiah Royce, and Charles Sanders Peirce*

Richard P. Mullin

State University of New York Press

Published by
State University of New York Press, Albany

For information, address State University of New York Press,
194 Washington Avenue, Suite 305, Albany, NY 12210-2384

Production by Judith Block
Marketing by Michael Campochiaro

Library of Congress Cataloging-in-Publication Data

Mullin, Richard P., 1939–
    The soul of classical American philosophy : the ethical and spiritual insights of
William James, Josiah Royce, and Charles Sanders Peirce / Richard P. Mullin.
        p. cm.
    Includes bibliographical references and index.
    ISBN-13: 978-0-7914-7109-8 (hardcover : alk. paper)
    ISBN-13: 978-0-7914-7110-4 (pbk.: alk. paper)
    1. Philosophy, American—19th century. 2. Philosophy, American—20th century.
3. James, William, 1842–1910. 4. Royce, Josiah, 1855–1916. 5. Peirce, Charles S.
(Charles Sanders), 1839–1914. I. Title.

B935.M85 2007
191—dc22

2006025533

10 9 8 7 6 5 4 3 2 1

To Marian

Contents

Introduction

In describing the soul of American Philosophy, this work presents three key figures who created magnificent philosophical works in the last part of the nineteenth and the early part of the twentieth centuries, the era of classical American Pragmatism. It features William James (1842–1910), Josiah Royce (1855–1916), and Charles Sanders Peirce (1839–1914), and focuses on the thought of these three philosophers as they dealt with issues that would be treated under the name of *soul* in traditional philosophy. These issues include: the search for truth; the meaning of whatever we call our "self," especially in relation to our bodily existence; free will; moral values; community, and our relationship with the Transcendent.

Purpose of this Work

This book has a twofold purpose. First, it aims to make the key ideas of these philosophers accessible to readers who are not specialists in this area or in philosophy in general. The book is relatively free of jargon and hopefully of all obscurity. It emphasizes the larger ideas rather than the knotty problems that often occupy philosophers when commenting on other philosophers. Second, it will not stress negative criticism with an eye to searching for short-comings, but rather it will illuminate the positive side of the ideas as they apply to thought and to life. As William James said of philosophy:

> Philosophy is at once the most sublime and the most trivial of human pur-suits. It works in the minutest crannies and opens the widest vistas...and repugnant as its manners, its doubting and challenging, its quibbling and dialectics, often are to common people, no one of us can get along without the far-flashing beams of light it sends over the world's perspectives.[1]

This work will look for the "far-flashing beams of light" and keep the quibbling to a minimum.

People often misunderstand pragmatism. In conversation, they often associate it with a lack of principle that permits anyone to do whatever seems expedient. This description does not fit the lives or the philosophical thought of the philosophers who invented and developed pragmatism. Of the philosophers presented in this book, James and Royce led exemplary lives. Peirce stumbled early in life, but his moral, social, and financial mistakes did not result from lack of principle; his mistakes were ironically due to a lack of practical sense. In the last decade of his life, however, he comported himself as a loving husband to his wife, who suffered chronic poor health, and the two lived in extreme poverty as Peirce dedicated himself to the work that he believed God created him to do. Each of these three philosophers gave ethics top priority.

The reputation of pragmatism suffers distortion not only from popular misconceptions, but also from contemporary philosophers who write under the banner of neo-pragmatism.[2] The project of the classical pragmatists was to re-think the issues of knowledge, truth, and value. Some neo-pragmatists rejected these as having no basis in reality, and they developed a view based on relativism and subjectivism. This book does not propose to analyze or evaluate the neo-pragmatists, but to clearly present the vision of the classical pragmatists.

The essential characteristic of pragmatism abides in the conviction that our actions follow from our beliefs. The only propositions that we really believe are those that we are willing to act on. This philosophy produced as its main outcome, a worldview that is scientific without being materialistic and reductionist, and which gives a proper place to the communal and spiritual aspects of human existence.

The late nineteenth and early twentieth centuries were marked by a decline in traditional religion, by a rapidly expanding industrialization, an increasing hold of science and technology over the minds of educated people, the centrality of Darwinian evolution to the worldview of intellectuals, and a sense of the futility of philosophy. These factors called into question the ability of the human person to believe in free will, the idea of community as anything other than a network of economic relations, and any meaning of human existence beyond acquisitive materialism. The pragmatists attempted to fill the intellectual and spiritual void. They created an interlocking, although sometimes conflicting, constellation of worldviews that integrate the progress in science with deeper and more general human needs. Nevertheless, the problems which they addressed continue to plague industrial and post-industrial society, and I will argue that these philosophers' insights continue to be part of the solution of our problems.

Charles Peirce's method, which he called "pragmatism," emphasizes the active role of the self in thinking and knowing. He rejects the notion of the mind as a passive spectator that receives clear and distinct ideas. His notion of the self connects closely to his method because the mind does not function apart from the self with its interests and plans. At a time when most scientists and philosophers saw the world as determined by mechanistic necessity, Peirce affirmed the reality of chance events and taught that the purpose of scientific thinking and all other thinking is to organize the world into an order favorable for survival and growth of the thinker. This task does not take place in solipsistic loneliness, but in community with other thinkers. Peirce defined truth as the belief which a community of investigators is destined to agree to in the long run.

William James adopted the method of pragmatism, which he used for testing the meaning of all ideas including scientific and philosophical ideas. He defined a true idea as one that enables the person who accepts it to get in touch with reality. He saw reality as a "semi-chaos" which is somewhat malleable and can, to some extent, bend to the interests of the thinking and acting person. We humans create our world by our interaction with reality. But we cannot create it any way we wish, because reality acts as a constraint to which we must yield. And yet several possible worlds can be created out of the same reality, depending partly on our evolutionary and cultural inheritance, and partly on our own interests. Free will means that we can choose what we pay attention to and thereby choose our actions and to some extent our world. The concept of free will takes a central place in James's personal life as well as in his philosophy. James took on as his intellectual and moral ideal the task of establishing a "republic of ideas" in which we would never consider a philosophical or ethical system finished until all persons have had their say.

Many descriptions of American pragmatists do not include Josiah Royce who identified himself as a philosophical idealist. However, the founder of the pragmatist movement, Charles Peirce, referred to Royce as the only true American pragmatist other than himself.[3] Like James, Royce subordinated the importance of intellectual knowing to acts of the human will. Individuals define themselves by the plans and purposes that they fulfill. The idea of community, by which he hoped to overcome the destructiveness of conflicting forces by creating "one out of many" stands as the goal of Royce's philosophy. He believed that the idea of community could overcome the one-sidedness of both individualism and collectivism. Every sphere of human life needs community. For example, in philosophy and science, Royce, like Peirce, believed that the search for knowledge requires a community of investigators who hold the pursuit of objective truth as their first priority.

Most histories of American pragmatism list John Dewey as one of the principle figures. Without denying his importance, this book will emphasize the three philosophers described above. Dewey's instrumentalism allies closely with the pragmatism of James, but emphasized the biological context of thought more than the other pragmatists. All thinking takes place in the interaction between an organism and its environment. Dewey attempted to overcome dichotomies such as that between mind and matter and between means and ends. He contended that all thought has roots in immediate experience, and he denied a separate sphere of pure reason and preestablished ends. Social and moral problems reflect bad adjustments to the changing environment and result from ignorance and poor thinking. The human self is essentially social in that all thinking takes place in a social context. All organizations, whether they are social, political, economic, religious, or educational should be evaluated by whether or not they promote personal freedom and growth. John Dewey stands out among the most important classical pragmatists and his work receives adequate and deserved attention.

Personal Note

When I first began graduate work in philosophy at Duquesne University, I was, like many of my generation, fascinated by European existentialists and phenomenologists. When I began teaching these ideas to undergraduates at a small college in Alabama, I felt like I was running my motor but not going anywhere. The students found the ideas entertaining, but when they asked what the point was, I did not have a good answer. I found myself agreeing with Abraham Maslow's comment that much of this philosophy amounted to "High I.Q. whimpering on a cosmic scale."

By contrast, when I taught William James I felt like I had shifted into gear. During a summer in Pittsburgh, I attended a doctoral defense by a friend at Duquesne. His dissertation dealt with Nietzsche, and although it represented first rate scholarship, it made for a very depressing way to spend an afternoon. But the presenter said something that changed my life. As he sighed and stooped beneath the burden of his own thought, he said: "You become what you read." I resolved that day to spend a lot of time reading William James and changed my dissertation topic from a French phenomenologist to William James. I now consider William James to be my principal teacher of philosophy.

In the late 1980s I took an interest in Yugoslavia and especially Slovenia. I arranged to meet the chair of the philosophy department of the University of Ljubljana and got an invitation to go there and lecture on American philosophy. This caused me to delve deeper than I had ever before into Peirce and Royce. I went to Slovenia in November 1991, shortly after it had gained its independence from the moribund federation of Yugoslavia, and again in

1993. In 1996, I went to Slovakia to give a series of lectures at the newly reconstituted University of Trnava. Trnava is a state university with a Catholic orientation, an institution that was not possible under a Communist Czechoslovakia. The administrators were surprised to learn that American pragmatism is compatible with Christianity. I told them that this misunderstanding prevails among Americans as well. I suggested to my hosts that the work of James, Royce, and Peirce, coming from outside the Catholic tradition, could serve to revitalize Catholic philosophy in a way analogous to the way the works of Aristotle did in the thirteenth century. In fact, I think that philosophy as a whole can be regenerated by a deep drink from the spring of classical American pragmatism. Students who study these ideas will be lifted to a higher level in their own thinking. It is with this hope that I write this book.

Abbreviations

Works by William James

ERE   *Essays in Radical Empiricism and A Pluralistic Universe.* Gloucester, MA: Peter Smith, 1967.

HI   Human Immortality, published with *The Will to Believe and Other Essays on Popular Philosophy.* NY: Dover Publications, 1956.

Prag.   *Pragmatism and the Meaning of Truth.* Cambridge, MA: Harvard University Press, 1978.

PP   *Principles of Psychology.* New York: Dover Publications, 1950.

EFM   *Essays in Faith and Morals,* selected by Ralph Barton Perry. New York: Longmans Green, 1949.

VRE   *Varieties of Religious Experience.* New York: New American Library, 1958.

WB   *The Will to Believe and Other Essays on Popular Philosophy.* New York: Dover Publications, 1956.

Works by Charles Sanders Peirce

CP   *Collected Papers.* Cambridge, MA: Harvard University Press. Electronic Version, InteLex Corporation.

Works by Josiah Royce

PL   *The Philosophy of Loyalty.* Nashville: Vanderbilt University Press, 1995.

PC   *The Problem of Christianity.* Washington, DC: the Catholic University of America Press, 2001.

SRI   *The Sources of Religious Insight.* New York: Charles Scribners Sons, 1912.
SGE   *Studies of Good and Evil: A Series of Essays upon the Problems of Philosophy and Life.* Hamden, CT: Archon Books, 1964.
WI   *The World and the Individual.* Glouchester, MA: Peter Smith, 1976.

Part I

William James

Chapter 1

Meaning and Truth

Pragmatism

William James described *pragmatism* as a method of approaching meaning and truth that would overcome the split between scientific and religious thinking. Scientific and religious thought had developed in isolation from each other and each resides in a particular temperament. James called the scientific approach "tough-minded" and pointed out that its adherents tend to be empiricist, determinist, materialist, and pessimistic. The "tender-minded" personality tends to be idealist, believes in free will and the reality of spiritual beings, and has an optimistic outlook. James did not assert that truth depends on temperament but that the kind of proposition that a person more likely *accepts* as true, depends on temperament. The pragmatic method was intended to bridge the gap between the tough- and tender-minded by discerning the meaning and truth-value of any proposition regardless of the temperament of the person who advocates it.

James attributed the origin of pragmatism to his friend, Charles Sanders Peirce. In his essay, "How to Make our Ideas Clear," Peirce's starting point was a critique of Rene Descartes. Peirce charged that Descartes offered clarity as the criterion for true ideas, but he did not explain what constitutes a clear idea, or prescribe how we can make our ideas clear. As the title of Peirce's essay implies, he hoped to remedy the omission he found in Descartes. Peirce suggested that in beginning philosophy, we should dismiss "make-believe" methods such as Descartes' methodic doubt. Instead, there is only one place from which we can begin, namely, the place in which we find ourselves when we begin. If we look at our minds at any moment, we find two kinds of thoughts, beliefs and doubts. A doubt identifies a state of mind in which we need to ask a question. A belief is a state of mind in which we can make a statement. Doubt involves uneasiness due to a lack of a rule to determine our action. We do not know what to do aside from clearing up the doubt by finding an answer to the question. We clear up the doubt by "fixing," that is, establishing a belief. A belief is a rule of action. When we have a belief, we know what we would do, given the proper circumstances. We act on our beliefs; otherwise they are not really beliefs. The fundamental principle of pragmatism teaches that we can truly say that we believe a proposition only if we are willing to act on it. The meaning of any belief is precisely the kind of action to which it leads. We make an idea clear therefore, by identifying the action that we would perform if we believe the idea, and the result that would follow if the idea is true.

William James developed pragmatism into a method for determining the meaning and testing the truth of any proposition. Pragmatism means the belief that the whole meaning of any proposition shows itself in the difference that results if the proposition holds true. If anyone asserts anything whatsoever, the pragmatist asks, "So what? What difference will it make in anyone's life if the proposition is true?" That difference constitutes the whole meaning of the proposition. If believing the proposition makes no difference, the proposition is meaningless. When a dispute breaks out the pragmatist asks, "What difference will it make if this or that position stands as the correct one?" If no difference results, the dispute is merely verbal.

According to the pragmatic theory of meaning, ideas are a way to adapt to the environment, that is, to solve problems. The human mind develops abstract concepts that substitute for perceptions and images. The formation of concepts enables us to apply the experience of the past to a wide range of problems and to anticipate problems that have not yet appeared. We have many concepts that we never actually use to solve problems. Just as nature provides an extravagant number of organisms, so human nature extravagantly allows for a large number of concepts that each person is able to master. Nature exhibits, as an operating principle, that in order to assure a sufficient supply of anything we have to have an overabundance. So although many of our concepts are not actually useful to us, concepts as a whole have a practical purpose.

James developed his theory of meaning into a theory of truth. The only things that can be called true or false are beliefs. Reality is not true; it simply is. A belief holds true if it agrees with reality. This formula sounds like the traditional correspondence theory of truth. But James carries it further by asking what it means for an idea to correspond to reality. Sometimes it could mean to copy, as, for example, when I have a mental picture of my wife that corresponds to what she really looks like. When I meet her, for instance, at an airport I recognize her. But most of the time our concepts do not copy reality. For example, our concepts of chemistry or economics are not copies.

We can make true statements about molecular models or supply and demand curves without imagining that they copy the physical or economic world.

What does it mean, then, to say that our concepts correspond to reality? They correspond if they lead us to a satisfactory relationship with reality. Truth is a *leading*. James provides an anecdote to illustrate the meaning of truth as a leading. A lone hiker in the mountains gets lost and feels tired, cold, hungry, and scared. But then he discovers a path, sees evidence of cows, and concludes that he has come upon a cow path and at the end of it he will find a farmhouse. He follows the path to safety. His idea of the cow path validates itself as true because it leads him to where he thought it would. James sees this incident as a prototype of a true idea because all true ideas lead to what we expect. Any false idea will lead us astray or at least to some unexpected aspect of reality. The ideas of the physicist or chemist, for example, hold true to the extent that they enable the scientist to predict or manipulate reality. We evaluate our common sense ideas in the same way. For example, if we take the ideas by which we find our way around a city or plan a career, they hold true to the extent that they lead us to where we want to go.

While not every belief demonstrates this theory of truth as clearly as the cow path, James holds that all of our beliefs, common sense, scientific, ethical, metaphysical, or religious, have their basis ultimately on this verification process. Although most of our beliefs will never be personally *verified*, they hold true in that they are *verifiable*. A hiker who is not lost may come upon the cow path and not follow it. Yet he believes truly that a house stands at the end of it. This belief is not useful at the time, but could be useful in a future emergency. To say that a belief holds true means that it could lead to an actual verification whether it has in fact done so or not.

The definition of truth, which was developed for the sensible order, also applies to the ideal order. James considered mental relations such as mathematical systems to be real. Just as true ideas of facts can lead us successfully through concrete reality, so true ideas of principles can lead us through abstract reality. False ideas in the abstract order will fail just as false ideas in the perceptual order will fail. In each case, false ideas lead to inconsistency and frustration. As James sums up the importance of truth in the ideal order, "We can no more play fast and loose with these abstract relations than we can with our sense experience. They coerce us: we must treat them consistently whether or not we like the results" (*Prag*, 101).

Radical Empiricism

James's pragmatic theory of meaning and truth was supplemented by his theory of "radical empiricism," which not only clarified some issues regarding our understanding, but also provided content for his view of reality. In the language of philosophy, he not only clarified some epistemological issues, but also provided metaphysical content as well. James was an empiricist through and through and rejected the notion that we can begin philosophy with abstract concepts. All of our knowledge comes to us in the stream of experience that flows continuously. In our concepts, we break the stream into pieces and freeze it as we do when we take photographic snap-shots of an action scene. A concept consists of a static and discrete bit of mental consciousness that intends to represent a part of the continuous stream of consciousness. For example, such simple concepts as "lake" or "forest" represent tremendous moving streams teeming with life.

James's radical empiricism differs from the traditional empiricism of John Locke, George Berkeley, and David Hume because these British philosophers thought that the basic experience consists of a simple idea such as blue or soft. James observed that we experience relationships as primordially as we do the so-called primary and secondary qualities of things. For example, we experience blue in the changing context of a blue object such as a blue sky, a blue pen, or blueberry. The concept "blue" consists of an abstraction distilled from these experiences. Relations are also part of experience rather than mere conceptual tools for organizing experience. Experience flows as a stream that includes conjunctions, copulas, and prepositions as well as verbs, nouns, and adjectives.[1] To illustrate James's point, when we perceive a "mother and child," we perceive the relationship as immediately as the two individuals who make up the relationship. We can say the same of the perceptions of inanimate conjunctions such as "hills and valleys" or "wind and rain."

James's notion of radical empiricism holds that nothing should count for knowledge unless it is experienced, and everything that is experienced should count for knowledge. The traditional empiricism ignores experienced relationships and change because they do not fit the a priori belief that knowledge is composed of simple ideas. Locke thought that simple ideas reside somehow in our mind like soup cans in a cupboard. They enter the mind through the senses and become the building blocks for all of the more complex ideas. James, by contrast, pointed out that we experience the world first as part of the continuous flow, and then we develop static simple ideas.

To understand the connection between the pragmatic theory and the theory of radical empiricism, we need to examine the roll that concepts play in James's theory of knowledge. The emphasis on experience provides the reason for the pragmatic theory of meaning. To understand the priority of experience we need a closer look at concepts. At any given time when our attention focuses on concepts, as it does right now, these concepts constitute parts of experience. Take the example of a medical doctor who examines a child's throat and sees a discoloration that makes her think that the patient suffers from an infection. While she performs the examination, the patient may be squirming, and, of course, the symptoms of the infection make sense only in the context of a human throat. The doctor, the patient, and the infection all flow in the stream of experience. But when the doctor thinks about a diagnosis and prescription, she uses concepts, perhaps concepts of a particular bacterial infection and the most recent antibiotic. She knows the concepts as clear, distinct, and fixed. She could check them in a medical journal or describe them to a colleague. But even while actively thinking, she still flows in the stream of experience, and the concepts are part of the experience. The main epistemological question concerns the connection between the distinct static concepts and the part of reality to which they refer. That is, what constitutes the connection between the concept of a bacterial infection and the color that the doctor sees in the context of the squirming child?

In James's epistemological theory, concepts *represent* percepts. To say that they represent percepts means that they substitute for them; they take their place. When we want to think about an experience, we may think instead about a concept, which we intend to take the place of that percept. For example, in planning a trip, concepts of highways railroads and airports can take the place of actually traveling each of them. In choosing between two routes, we do not have to physically travel both before making a decision. We do not even have to go over each route in our imagination. A set of concepts that includes a flight number, time of departure, and destination substitutes for an enormous perceptual reality. If our beliefs about these concepts hold true, then by acting on them we arrive at our desired destination. Students and other readers often ask whether the ideas lead us because they hold true, or do they hold true because they lead us. For James, the *leading is the truth*. The effectiveness of concepts in leading to reality is what it means to say that the concepts hold true. The truth of a concept consists of its agreement with reality and our concepts agree with reality by leading us to the reality to which they refer.

The example of ideas leading to a geographical destination may seem commonplace and perhaps trivial. But it provides a clear analogy to the way that concepts lead us through the stream of experience to the experience that we seek. If a concept refers to no experience, and cannot conceivably lead us to any experience, and the truth or falsity of the concept makes no difference, then the concept is meaningless. The pragmatic axiom is that "there is no difference which does not make a difference." Aimless verbal disputes that people sometimes mistake for philosophical disputes are in fact meaningless.[2] There can be no difference between two concepts except that which makes a difference in how we relate to the perceptual world.

James illustrates his method with an explanation of human activity. In an essay titled "The Experience of Activity," James explicitly said that he would explain both the meaning of human activity and his method. He describes the pragmatic method in which we find the meaning of each idea by searching for its consequences. He calls radical empiricism a methodological postulate and defines it as follows: "Nothing shall be admitted as a fact except what can be experienced at some definite time by some experiment; and for every feature of fact ever so experienced, a definite place must be found somewhere in the final system of reality" (ERE, 160). The description of activity illustrates how the method of pragmatism and the postulate of radical empiricism fit together.

We can distinguish every activity as either aimless or directed. If directed, it may or may not be resisted. If it goes unresisted, we will usually carry it out without much thought. If it is resisted, we might quit or continue with effort. If we continue with effort, we may or may not overcome the resistance and achieve our intended purpose. The prototype of all activity in the universe shows itself in "this dramatic shape of something sustaining a felt purpose against felt obstacles and overcoming or being overcome" (ERE, 168).

The point of radical empiricism affirms that the felt activity can be taken as real. Reality includes the desire for the intended purpose, the rub of the obstacle, the decision to work against the obstacle with effort, the strain, and the final overcoming or being overcome. Our knowledge of causality flows from our subjective experience of effective activity. Radical empiricism states that these experiences cannot be thrown out of court simply on the grounds that they are subjective. We really do experience them and, because they are experienced, they have a place in an adequate understanding of reality. An explanation of what really happens must give an account of the purpose, the effort, the strain, and the triumph or defeat.

James's method can also be illustrated by the way he treats the relationship between the knower and the known. According to the hypothesis of radical empiricism, nothing that is not experienced may be included in a philosophical view, and nothing experienced may be excluded. It follows that knowledge requires that both the knower and the known must constitute parts of experience (ERE, 196). The relationship between knower and known itself stands as a portion of experience.

Conceptual knowledge constitutes the other way in which portions of experience can relate to each other as knower and known. Concepts make up parts of experience, and we experience them as knowledge of percepts or of other concepts. The concepts know the percepts by substituting for them. As in the example given above, the concept by which a person begins to plan a journey knows the whole flow of concepts and percepts, which conclude in the experience of arrival at the conceived destination. Concepts represent other parts of experience. We can distinguish concepts from the parts of experience that they represent and thereby we experience the distinction between knower and known.

To summarize James's methodological principles, namely, pragmatism and radical empiricism, concepts are portions of experience, and we find their meaning in the experienced concepts and percepts to which they lead. Concepts enable us to find our way through experience, which is continuous, always flowing, and abounding in chaos. We form concepts by abstracting from the stream of experience, isolating portions of it, and stopping the action. The concepts then substitute for large portions of experience. The "cash value" or *pragmatic meaning* of any concept resides in the percept that it leads us to expect and the actions that it enables us to prepare. An idea that has no such pragmatic meaning is meaningless. We find the *truth* of a meaningful idea in how well it leads us through experience. James's approach to meaning provides a unified theory that applies to all thought including common sense, science, and metaphysics.

Chapter 2

Body and Mind

To sort out what we can learn from James about the important issues of human life such as whether we have free will, whether we can join with others in real community, whether we can hope for life after death, and whether we can believe in God, we need as clear a view as possible on the meaning that James attributed to the mind and its relation to the body. We can understand James best by situating his position in the context of Western philosophy and comparing his thoughts to those that other philosophers have attributed to the concept of a "soul." The two most opposing ideas are the dualist notion that the soul constitutes the real self, which is immortal and temporarily housed in a body, compared to the notion that the soul is an illusion that can be explained away in terms of material neurons that make up the brain.

Materialism versus Dualism

Plato and Descartes exemplify dualism. Plato held that the soul preexists the body and survives after death. The task of philosophy is to liberate the soul from the limitations and impurities of bodily existence. In the dialogue *Phaedo,* when Socrates' friends ask how they should bury him, he makes it clear that "Socrates" will be gone when they bury the body. Rene Descartes in the seventeenth century argued that the conscious ego is a thinking thing while the body is an extended thing. These are two different kinds of sub-stance. The self has the capacity to think independently of the body or of bodily images.

The opposite view appeared first in ancient Greece in the thought of Democritus and the school that came to be known as "atomism." According to this view, reality consists of indivisible particles—atoms—that move in space and form visible things by aggregations. The body and what we call the soul are nothing but collections and arrangements of atoms, and when the arrangement dissolves, the body and soul are gone. This view reappeared in the seventeenth century, and with the later development of modern chemistry, it became the basis of scientific materialism. It has had many advocates and perhaps the most articulate today is Francis Crick. In his book, *The Astonishing Hypothesis,* he argues that "You are nothing but the behavior of a vast assembly of nerve cells and their associated behavior."[1] The nerve cells and their behavior depend on the action of the molecules that compose them. In principle, we can explain all behavior and all consciousness in terms of the molecules. We do not need a hypothesis of "the soul"; free will and immortality are illusions. Crick unabashedly calls himself a reductionist and points out that the success of all modern science depends on reduction of the wholes to the parts. The scientists of one hundred years ago, including James, would probably not have been astonished by Crick's hypothesis. Although Crick has much more information about molecular biology, he offers no surprises that would require a paradigm shift. Whether we look at materialism from the viewpoint of the crude atomism of Democritus or the sophisticated molecular science of Crick, the philosophical assumptions remain the same, namely, that to understand the material conditions of consciousness means to know consciousness. James dismissed the reductionists as those who believe that a Beethoven string quartet is *nothing but* the scraping of horse hairs on cat guts. We must now ask whether James successfully answered the challenge of the reductionists.

Before looking at James's approach to this issue, one more alternative should be mentioned although only briefly. Aristotle and St. Thomas held that the soul relates to the body as form to matter. A person consists of neither just a soul nor just a collection of material parts, but rather as composition of body and soul. The same self who understands the highest spiritual ideas is the very one who feels bodily pain and pleasure. This view is called *hylomorphism* from the Greek words *hyle* and *morphe,* which mean matter and form. From the materialist point of view, St. Thomas's notion of the soul would seem to slip into dualism. For although the soul serves as the form of the body, it has an operation—reason—that subsists independently of matter, and at death, it can survive without the body. While the comparison and distinction between hylomorphism and dualism makes a fascinating philosophical question, it cannot be taken up here. From the point of view of James as well as that of the materialists, hylomorphism may be classified with dualism. The view of William James differs from each of these three. The views of Josiah Royce and Charles Sanders Peirce, as we will see, are also different.

Neither Dualism nor Materialism

James offered a view that was neither dualistic nor materialistic. His understanding appears, at first, to be much more like that of the materialist than either a dualist or a hylomorphic philosopher. James believed that all thinking has a physiological base. He rooted his philosophy in experience, and experience does not reveal any pure thought separate from the body. On the contrary, his own investigations connected every thought to some bodily movement even if only a subtle motion of the muscles in the throat or forehead. He rejected dualism as a mistake based on the unawareness of the physiology of thinking (ERE, 37). This belief, taken alone, would place him solidly in the materialist camp. James, however, rejected materialism and asserted several beliefs incompatible with it. These include free will, human immortality, and what he called the "religious hypothesis"—that the best things are the eternal things. The question becomes whether James was consistent in rejecting both dualism and materialism.

James proposed that the ultimate reality consists of "pure experience," which consciousness splits into subject and object (ERE, 4). While the materialist believes that sensation and all other mental activity result from physical events, and the dualist believes that at least some mental acts stand independently of physical reality and exert causative influence, James saw physical events and mental acts as different aspects of pure experience. Controversy swirled around the meaning and feasibility of pure experience and the controversy continues to the present. Because the idea of pure experience remains questionable yet insightful and central to James's view of reality, we do well to look at it from the viewpoint of a critic to clarify it and to see if it can withstand the criticism. The critic that I choose is Gerald Myers, author of *William James, His Life and Work*, a critic who stands out because of his comprehensive knowledge of James and the clarity and power of his thinking.[2] Myers contends that "pure experience" represents a form of Berkeleyan idealism, which reduces physical reality to sensations. Berkeley had argued that "to be is to be perceived" meaning that the whole reality of an object consists in its being perceived. When we perceive an object as red and smooth, the whole reality of the object consists of its redness, smoothness, and whatever other qualities we perceive. There is no underlying substance that has these qualities. Only the qualities are real, and they are real in as much as they are perceived. Myers contends that James resorts to Berkeley's position as a way to save his metaphysics from materialism. According to Myers, the Berkeleyan position is untenable so James's attempt fails and with it, James's entire metaphysical project.

Myers cites a passage in *Principles of Psychology* in which James seems to reduce *things* to sensations. The passage appears in James's discussion of

Hermann Helmholtz who asserted that we notice only those sensations that are signs of things. James goes further and contends that [things are] "nothing but special groups of sensible qualities which happen practically or aesthetically to interest us, to which we therefore give substantial names and which we exalt to the status of independent dignity" (Myers, 319). Myers labels this view as phenomenalism or Berkeleyan idealism in that it defines physical things as mere collections of sensible qualities. He argues that it is difficult to defend this position on the premise of the *Principles of Psychology* where it is found, but that "it fits neatly into the scheme of radical empiricism where everything is made of sensations or sensible qualities" (Myers, 319).

For the purpose of this chapter, we need not question the consistency of *Principles of Psychology*, but we face a very important task of determining whether Myers correctly asserts that James's view of pure experience constitutes Berkeleyan idealism, and that it serves as the basis of radical empiricism. If both of these assertions can be answered affirmatively, this, along with the argument that Berkeleyan idealism is untenable, would undermine and discredit radical empiricism. Myers argues that in fact James's radical empiricism stands discredited.

Myers affirms the materialist view according to which electrons and protons cause the sensations such as red or smooth. The redness or the smoothness result from the physical reality but do not constitute reality itself. He portrays James as asserting that the physical thing is nothing but the sensation of redness or smoothness. Such a view is implausible because, if it were true, the outer world would disappear and becomes a projection of our inner world. Myers contends that James takes this position as a tactic to ward off materialism. He sums up his critique of James,

> Despite his claim that radical empiricism is neutral and that pure experiences are neither physical nor mental until associated into larger contexts, James seems to have tipped his hand. At stake for him as for Berkeley was whether physical things—which we normally consider utterly different from sensations—are in fact nothing but sensations at the core of our inner lives. (Myers, 320)

Myers points out that "The properties of physical things cannot be borne by sensations....Sensations do not flake, rust, corrode, fertilize or explode" (Myers, 320). Sensations are not properties of objects, but rather chemico-physical effects of the objects on nerve receptors. He wraps up his argument against the idealist interpretation saying,

> There is no way of plausibly conceiving physical things as analyzable only into tactile sensations and the like. Since this conception is what radical

empiricism proposes, it renders the vision of pure experience indefensible from the outset. (Myers, 320)

He concludes that James, in spite of his disclaimers, had reduced physical reality to subjective sensations.

Myers contends that James's motive for reducing things to sensations was to open up the possibility that consciousness is not totally dependent on our brain and that our inner life is part of a larger godlike consciousness. Independent consciousness is possible in a universe whose fundamental units are sensations rather than electrons and protons. In James's view, sensations are pulses in the experienced stream of consciousness. According to Myers's interpretation, James was misled by his desire to liberate his metaphysical views from the common belief of materialism "that everything, including sensations, are explicable by chemico-physical processes in which the sensations have no part" (Myers, 320). If, as Myers asserts, James reduces reality to sensations, then James's thesis remains implausible. How could the whole reality of fire, for example, be reduced to sensations of warmth, heat, or pain? But while this question seems to highlight an obvious problem it evokes a more difficult question, how could James hold such an implausible position? In fact, James presented many ways in which inner and outer experience differ and would certainly agree with Myers's comment that inner experiences including sensations "do not flake, rust, corrode, fertilize or explode."

James explicitly rejects the position of Berkeleyan idealism, namely, that we each know only our own experience.[3] He calls his own philosophy a "natural realism"[4] and insists that you and I see the same "Memorial Hall." If I look at you or touch your body, I see or touch the same body you feel from the inside and activate. But Myers supports his interpretation by pointing out that in the essay, "The Essence of Humanism," James said that experience is self-contained and there is no need for a transcendent substratum (Myers, 319). This statement, as Myers interprets it, reduces the world of solid objects along with their molecular structures to phenomena in the consciousness of the experiencer. In "Does Consciousness Exist?" James approvingly quotes Shadworth Hodgson's statement that each experience, for instance, of a desktop "is made of that, of just that experience of space, of brownness, flatness, heaviness, etc." (ERE. 27). This assertion appears to be a denial of the molecular structure that causes the experiences of brown, flat, and heavy.

James's vision presents such difficulty that James himself never gave an account that he found satisfying.[5] If Myers stands correct, James's treatment of "pure experience" as a way to avoid materialism while asserting non-dualistic naturalism fails. But perhaps an interpretation, different from that of Myers, could bring us closer to what James attempted. A more favorable explanation of James, so that he does not reduce reality to sensations that are part of our inner lives, requires that we set aside the entire framework within which Myers presents his critique. Myers holds that molecular structures cause subjective sensations and that James denies the molecular structures and so is left with subjective sensations. But James seems to have viewed reality very differently. When he says that experience leans only on experience and needs nothing outside of experience, he does not mean that reality exists only in the subjective sensations of one or several individuals. Rather he posits a self-contained continuity of actual *or potential* experience. James's view of continuity may be illustrated by a commonplace example. If a person loses his pen, he uses concepts to try to find it: "Where was I last using it? Where do I usually put it?" Then when he finds it, the percepts of finding and holding the pen fulfill the cognitive content of the concepts. No gaps exist in the spatial and temporal context of looking for a pen and finding it. The concepts are experiences, which lead to the perceptual experience of finding a pen. The concepts, though distinct in meaning, flow as part of the experiential stream of the seeker. The perceptual pen is the terminus ad quem of the search.

But now we might search for a more absolute reality and inquire about the molecular structure, which we would conceptually call the reality behind the appearance. The chemical concepts constitute experiences that substitute for a reality that we define in terms of a percept. James defined reality as "a terminus within the general possibilities of experience" (ERE, 201). For some purposes, we may call the pen real, for others, we say that the molecular structure is real. There is no contradiction, nor even a discontinuity, between the common sense perception of the pen and the chemist's analysis of it. Continuity also exists between my subjective experience of the pen, the objective reality of the pen, and your subjective experience of the pen. We need neither to reduce the world to objective atoms nor to subjective sensations. Concepts, percepts, and particles are continuous and potentially conterminous. The concepts of several people can lead to all of them perceiving the same object.

Another look at the quote by Shadworth Hodgson is in order. James agrees that each experience "is made of that, of just that experience of space, of intensity, of flatness, brownness, heaviness or what not." If we perceive a desk top, we experience brownness, flatness, heaviness, and so forth. In calling these real, James does not mean that the desk subsists only in our mind. Our sensations get us in touch with the real desk which any other person would also perceive. If we examine the desk physically and talk about mass and density instead of heaviness, we find continuity between these two ways of experiencing. In addition, if we examine the physiology of sensations, there is continuity between these physiological concepts and our visual and tactile experience. The "heaviness" in our mind is a concept and, of course, it does not bear the weight of the desk. But the concept of heaviness allows us to know what sensations to expect and what preparations to make if we wish to move the desk. When we lift the desk, our feeling of resistance is the same as the heaviness of the desk.

In his essay, "Does 'Consciousness' Exist?" James argues that conscious acts do not presuppose a distinct entity called "consciousness" that somehow relates to reality as knower to known. Instead, he maintains that knower and known express the same experience seen in two different contexts. He compares experience to a point at which two lines intersect. The same point can be regarded as a point on either line while remaining just one point. So we may perceive an object such as the wall of the room we happen to be in while writing or lecturing. According to James's argument, the wall that we perceive and the wall itself are identical. We need postulate neither a mysterious thing-in-itself nor a transcendental consciousness. But we *speak* of the difference between the room and our consciousness of the room. In fact, we *experience* this difference. The room endures long after we are gone, and our memory of the room lacks the clarity and consistency of the room itself. Other people will experience the room, and we will experience other things.

James contended that the distinction between knower and known comes about through addition of different sets of related experiences to the original experience. We can take the perceptual experience of a room and relate it to the history of the building, or we can look at it in the context of the biography of the person who perceives it. In this way, we count the same experience twice, and we distinguish the known building from the knower. The outcome of the analysis of knower and known is that pure experience does not express Berkeleyan idealism but rather represents a non-dualistic alternative to materialism. In clarifying this key concept James states:

> 'Pure experience' is the name which I gave to the immediate flux of life, which furnishes the material to our later reflection with its conceptual categories. Only new-born babes, or men in semi-coma from sleep, drugs, illnesses, or blows, may be assumed to have an experience pure in the literal sense of a *that* which is not yet a *what* tho' ready to be all sort of whats. (ERE, 93)

The human organism transforms "the big blooming buzzing confusion" into a self-conscious mind and it object. The distinction of mind and matter result from the bifurcation of pure experience. James considered himself a realist but believed that reality is undetermined and therefore open to various interpretations. He held that reality can not be limited to the physico-chemical structure, as we understand it.

James does not reduce physical matter to sensations as Myers claims he does. Physical properties and sensations are different aspects of pure experience. Pure experience occurs in a field of primal reality that flows as a continuum. The human organism identifies thought as separate from the object in the act of self-consciousness. Prior to this, they coexist as potential parts of a continuum. To try to know pure experience directly imitates the child who opens the refrigerator door very quickly to see if the light really goes off when the door is closed. As soon as we try to observe pure experience, it becomes ordinary experience with its components of subject and object. Since "pure experience" remains unknown, could James have avoided misunderstanding by calling it "pure reality?" Calling it "pure experience" tips it to the subjective side instead of being neutral. I think he could have achieved his purpose by saying that human experience divides "pure reality" into the natural world of both commons sense and science, and the world of our conscious percepts and concepts.

The practical difference between James' position and that of a materialist and a dualist may be illustrated by taking an example of an apparent act of free will. In the *Principles*, James describes the ideo-motor theory of action and argues that the idea that dominates the mind will control the way the body reacts to stimuli. The idea of free will poses the question of whether or not we can choose which idea dominates. Can we attend to one set of ideas when we might have attended to another, especially when we have a natural propensity to one of the options? James contends that this happens every time we experience effort. We exert effort every time we choose to pay attention to an abstract thought when it competes with whatever is instinctive.

James takes, as the prototype of an act of the will, the act of getting out of bed on a cold morning. A materialist contends that neurons cause the action of getting out of bed, as well as our consciousness of some purpose for getting up. A dualist position would be that we have some nonmaterial purpose that somehow triggers the neurons to obey it. James on the other hand holds that the organism, which has conflicting interests—staying warm versus its interest in the day's work—turns from the former to the latter and we get out of bed. The structure of this act, from the time that our consciousness shifts from the comfort of the bed to a reverie of the day's activity to the point at which we are out of the bed, involves the whole range of physiological as well as phenomenological changes. They are part of a whole, which we may later analyze from one point of view or the other. If we suffer damage on either side, neural damage or loss of meaning, we might not get up at all. A healthy brain is a necessary condition for thinking or acting. But it does not follow that we can reduce thought to brain activity or that brain activity is a sufficient cause of thought.

Thus, the gate stands open to the possibility that our individual consciousness is an aspect of a larger consciousness. The world of pure experience is not uncanny like the materialist view that leaves the world a dead "it." Nor is it ghostly like the world of dualism. James's view neither strips the body of spiritual meaning nor does it take the muscle and blood from the human spirit. Thought and action are analyzable parts, which initially belong to the integral life of the human organism.

A Radical Empiricist View of Mind and Body

What is the world like if radical empiricism is an adequate description? In the essay "Reflex Action and Theism," James shows that the human mind constructs a world from the infinite number of possibilities given in immediate sense experience. We construct the world as we understand it from the given contents of our impressions. Our minds perform the construction in the service of our volitional nature. As James says, "The conceiving or theorizing faculty—the mind's middle compartment—functions exclusively for the sake of ends that do not exist at all in the world of impressions we receive from our senses, but are set by our emotional and practical subjectivity altogether."[6] We take a given state of affairs and try to remake it into a state of affairs demanded by our volitional nature. But in what he calls the miracle of miracles, the given order bends, at least somewhat, to our desires and our efforts to remodel it. The scientist, the artist, and the person of practical affairs share the belief that the world will respond to their action if it is the right action. If they fail, they try again. They assume that "the impressions of sense must give way, must be reduced to the desiderated form. They all postulate in the interest of their volitional nature a harmony between the latter and the nature of things. The theologian does no more" (WB, 120). So, according to James, neither materialistic determinism nor free will is *given* in sense experience. Each expresses a way of trying to satisfy our human need for a rational world and each may be true to the extent that it satisfies our human need while accounting for what is given in reality.

I have attempted to show that James presented a worldview that avoids both dualism and materialism. He rejected dualism because the idea of thinking apart from the bodily organism stands contrary to all experience. But he also rejected materialism because it would exclude from possibility some aspects of reality which experience confirms, notably belief in free will. Radical empiricism asserts that pure experience constitutes the matrix from which we derive our ordinary experience of both mind and matter. Contrary to Myers, who contends that James denies matter by reducing it to the sensations of the person experiencing it, I have tried to show that James's notion of pure experience is a fundamental reality from which all ordinary experience, private or public, mental or physical is derived. Finally, I pointed out that

James's view of the world is one that can be rational to the scientist, artist, business leader, or theologian.

The acceptance of any worldview hinges on whether we believe that the world so viewed makes a congenial home to the rational mind. James calls the most rational view the one most compatible with experience, most logically consistent, and best able to meet the demands of our volitional nature. James argues that radical empiricism, with its notion of pure experience, accounts for objective reality as it is presented in the physical sciences, the experienced unity of body and mind, and the experience of free will. Compared to the possible alternatives—materialism, dualism, and idealism—the concept of pure experience best meets the criterion for a rational worldview that explains thinking as physiologically based and free.

Chapter 3

Free Will

The most important practical issue that flows from the view of mind and body relationship is that of free will. If we are physiologically determined so that the mind is a mere epiphenomenon—the mind is a product of brain activity but has no control over it—then free will is an illusion. Chapter 2 showed that James rejected the materialist view that would make free will an illusion and presented a view of reality and of the human person that makes it possible for human beings to take an active role in their own lives rather than that of a spectator. This chapter will look specifically at the issue of free will as James presented it and comment on how his ideas stand today.

The question of free will stands out as one of the most concrete and practical that anyone can ask. The question may be framed like this: "Can I, by effort, make the rest of my life significantly different from what it would be without that effort?" We can ignore the question when we are in the flow of things. When we are doing what we want to be doing, the question of free will does not impose itself, just as we ordinarily do not think about breathing unless we are having trouble breathing. But the question of free will becomes immensely important during crises in our life, whether they are caused by events closing in, or ourselves growing out. A theory of free will that flows in harmony with James's pragmatic theory of meaning must have practical consequences. In what follows, I will show that the theory of free will can serve as both a motivator and a program for becoming more free.

Psychology and the Subjective Experience of Free Will

In his *Principles of Psychology*,[1] James begins his analysis with the ideo-motor theory of behavior. Every state of mind connects to some bodily behavior. States of mind necessarily lead to action; for example, the sight of food will lead a hungry person to reach for it; the sight of a dangerous object such as a speeding car will cause him to jump up on the curb. As I am sitting at my computer working on these thoughts, I can look away from my monitor and see the lamp, the books, the pictures, and the window, and I anticipate a challenge to this theory. These visual ideas fill my mind, but they do not lead to any action. But then I look back at the monitor and at my notes, and I resume writing. The idea of writing about James and his theory of free will persists as the idea that prevails in my mind at the present, and it calls for some action on my part.

The simple relation of mental states to action does not constitute voluntary action. States of mind often lead to actions, which are merely reflexive such as brushing away a fly as soon as we become aware of it. Other actions may be compulsive escapes, such as paging through an old magazine when we become bored. The discussion of free will obviously requires more than just connecting action to a state of mind.

James defined an act of the will as the desire for some end that we believe to be in our power to achieve. Desires for ends that we do not consider attainable, remain mere *wishes*. At first glance this definition seems to fall short. A person often desires things that he believes lie within reach but does not will them. For example, I may wish to stop writing so that I can watch a football game on TV, but I *will* to keep writing. James explains this apparent difficulty by the description of inhibitions. If we desire two things that are incompatible, each inhibits the other. Sometimes the desire to write effectively inhibits the desire to watch a football game and sometimes the reverse happens. A person with only one desire would follow it inevitably. But since most of us have a plethora of conflicting desires, we follow only those that have the upper hand over their opponents.

Muscular movement constitutes the point of contact between our conscious states and our effect in the real world. These movements constitute the only immediate experience of an outward effect of our will. James argued that consciousness always acts impulsively, or inhibitively, that is, it tends to produce or restrain muscular movements. When a particular state of consciousness prevails, it will produce the action to which it tends. The question of voluntary action centers on how a given state of consciousness comes to prevail.

The states of mind that ordinarily have impulsive power include instinctive reactions such as emotions and appetites, ideas of pleasure and pain, ideas that we have developed the habit of obeying, and ideas that represent objects close to us in time and space. Since we usually find these states of mind as given rather than chosen, they do not constitute acts of free will. James summarizes the strong hold that such objects have on our attention:

"Compared with these various objects, all far off considerations, all highly abstract conceptions, unaccustomed reasons, and motives foreign to the instinctive history of the race, have little or no impulsive power" (*PP II*, 536). Reason speaks as a small voice, which may be heard, but is generally not followed. But reason *can* prevail. The factor that enables it to prevail against the stronger instinctive motives provides the key to understanding the effectiveness of freely chosen ideas.

This key is *effort*. We experience effort as the attempt to follow the line of greater resistance. The line of least resistance favors our instinctive and habitual inclinations. Our ideals do not have the strength of our inclinations. But effort steps up as an active force, which can combine with ideas and enable them to prevail over inclinations.

The effort that plays a crucial role in empowering ideal impulses is the effort to pay *attention* to them. James rejected the idea, popular in his time, that desire for pleasure and avoidance of pain exclusively determine behavior. He held that the impulsive or inhibiting power of an object depends on how *interesting* it is. Pleasurable things prove interesting, but things may be interesting for other reasons such as being painful or morbidly fascinating, or things may be interesting just because they are loud, colorful, or intense. Any object, which interests us enough to hold our attention, will have a decisive effect on our behavior, either as an impulse or inhibition. The questions evoked by James's analysis are these: What makes one object interesting enough to hold our attention over another? And, does the interest come from the object or from us? If an object such as a loud noise or intense feeling grabs our attention, our yielding to it does not provide an example of a free choice. But, with effort, a person can ignore intense impressions as, for example, a basketball player may concentrate on a free throw in spite of the taunting of the home crowd. When attention to an object requires effort, that attention can be called active or voluntary attention.

If the above description stands correct, volition can be defined as attention with effort. James gathers these considerations into a definition: "*The essential achievement of the will, in short, when it is most 'voluntary', is to ATTEND to a difficult object and hold it fast before the mind*" (*PP II*, 561; emphasis in original). A difficult object is one that we cannot pay attention to without effort. Strength of will consists of the ability to pay attention to the quiet voice of reason when it contradicts impulses or inhibitions that are naturally stronger than itself. Since the mind does not naturally attend to a non-instinctive idea for a long time, the effort must be constantly renewed. Effort picks up momentum as other ideas associated with the main idea begin to take their place in the mind, and the entire chain of ideas becomes habitual. If the effort can be renewed long enough, the idea will fill the mind and lead to the appropriate kind of activity.

Indeterminism and the Physical Possibility of Free Will

After giving an account of the subjective experience of free will, James defers the question of the objective freedom of the will because freedom considered objectively constitutes a metaphysical question and cannot be answered within the limits of his *Principles of Psychology*. He took up the question of freedom in his philosophical writings especially in his essay, "The Dilemma of Determinism." Determinism refers to the view that every event, including the neural activities associated with human thought, is determined by an unbroken chain of molecular activity. This view won common acceptance by the scientists of James's time. In *Pragmatism*, James listed determinism as one of the features of the "tough-minded" scientific mentality. But in "The Dilemma of Determinism" he argued that "indeterminism" proves to be a more rational view than determinism, and that free will is possible in an indeterminist universe. Indeterminism means that possibilities exceed actualities and that the past does not completely determine the future. The parts of the universe fit together loosely so that alternative futures are really possible, and this possible future or that one may become an actuality.

James bases the rationality of indeterminism on the existence of what he calls "judgments of regret." The argument, in short, is that we human beings in fact regret things; we deeply wish that past human acts, our own or others' were different from their reality. These judgments make sense only on the condition that people could possibly have acted the preferred way rather than the way that evokes the regret. James illustrates the fact of regret with a newspaper account of a man who cruelly murdered his wife. In a determinist universe, it would not make sense to regret that the man committed this crime, because he could not have done otherwise. All of our moral judgments would be irrational because neither we nor others could ever act otherwise than the way we do. Our entire moral sense would be an irrational illusion. James did not say that a universe in which we harbor an irrational moral sense is impossible. He argued simply that such a universe does not compel our belief. When we are faced with two possible but incompatible propositions, we are within our rights to believe the more rational of the two. Since an indeterminist view makes morality rational, we can reasonably believe that it is the correct view.

The prominent British analytical philosopher, A. J. Ayer (1910–1989), made a twentieth-century counterattack against this argument. Ayer claimed that an indeterminist universe is neither more rational nor more conducive to a moral view than is a determinist universe. According to Ayer's argument, even if there were chance events in the universe, they would not provide an argument for freedom and responsibility. For we are no more free if our actions are a result of chance than if they are the result of necessity. We would be nature's playthings instead of nature's slaves.[2]

But James's concept of freedom can survive this attack. Certainly if a human choice consists of nothing but a random firing of neurons, which the acting person cannot control, then the person does not choose freely, and Ayer's criticism makes a direct hit. But if an undetermined future waits, freedom has some room to work. Our ideas might not prevail, but more importantly, they *might*. To say that chance has a role in the physical universe does not mean that conscious acts flow from mere chance. Consciousness constitutes the realm of purpose, and the human story involves the imposition of purpose on matter in much the same way as Plato's demiurge struggles to create a cosmos out of chaos. Freedom consists of the prevailing of conscious purpose over reality as we find it. Matter resists the purposeful activity of consciousness and yet remains somewhat malleable. If a person chooses purposefully in terms of his or her ideals, and the choice determines, at least to some extent, which neural pathways are activated, then the person is to that extent free and not merely a slave or a plaything of nature. Indeterminism means that physical forces do not completely determine the physiological mechanism involved in making a decision. If a gap opens in the physical determinism of our brain, then conscious purpose can fill the gap and be a factor in determining the outcome of the thought process. Physiologically it may be undetermined whether a student spends an evening hanging out with friends or writing a philosophy paper, although the odds may be stacked somewhat in favor of the former. But since there remains some chance of it going the other way, the student can remind himself or herself of future hopes and past mistakes and so enable the more difficult idea to prevail.

Ayer's criticism of indeterminism has some force if it is applied to Jean-Paul Sartre's theory of freedom instead of James's theory. Sartre, in his analysis of anguish, uses the example of the mountain climber on a precipice who experiences vertigo because he does not know what freedom will choose in the next moment, and for all he knows, he may decide to jump; or the person who is unsure whether he will start shouting obscenities at any moment because freedom is free and makes new choices each moment.[3] The vulnerability of Sartre's idea as cited here shows by contrast that James's idea of freedom is immune from Ayer's attack. Sartre's background was a world of fantasy where anything can happen. James's background was scientific physiology. Habits are indelibly carved in the neural pathways. Habit will prevent a person from an extemporaneous decision to jump off a cliff or to shout obscenities in a classroom. Habits enable us to make promises and to work for the fulfillment of purposes. But we have to make the effort, and that comes neither from necessity nor chance. We can make the effort if, and only if, we choose to.

The discussion of indeterminism and physiology deals with the external manifestations of free will. James argued, successfully, I believe, that the subjective feeling of free will need not be an illusion. But the only experience of free will available is that which each of us has internally. The internal characterization of free will holds whether the experience manifests real power, as James argues, or is merely an illusion as the determinists argue. The previous chapter mentioned James's description of getting out of bed on a cold New England morning. A person may carry on a battle between the duty to get up and the desire to stay in the warm bed. As long as the battle goes on, the desire for comfort wins. The more we think about getting up, the stronger the inhibition against it becomes. As a motivating force, duty does not have a prayer. In James's analysis, we finally get up without any decision at all. As he describes it,

> We suddenly find that we have got up. A fortunate lapse of consciousness occurs. We forget both the warmth and the cold; we fall into some reverie connected with the day's life. At a lucky instant an idea of getting up flashes across our mind that does not awaken any inhibiting impulse and so its appropriate motor effect takes place. (PP II, 524–525)

Getting out of bed is not necessarily an act of free will. Even if we presuppose indeterminism, the cause of our getting up was a "lucky instant," and Ayer's criticism holds true. Given the fact that most of us get up every morning, the determinist thesis would seem much more plausible; we get up in the morning as most mammals do because that is how our neurons act. The question of free will in this case is the question of whether or not we could, with effort, attend to the idea of getting up, and make it prevail rather than it being a fortunate lapse of consciousness.

A Late Twentieth-Century Adaptation of James's Concept of Free Will

Psychologist Rollo May contends that there is a gap in James's description because he lived and wrote too soon to benefit from the insights of psychoanalysis and phenomenology.[4] May concedes that Freud exposed the Victorian notion of free will as illusion, but he does not accept the Freudian criticism uncritically. May sees the Victorian emphasis on conscious will and the Freudian rejection of the effectiveness of consciousness as a pair of one-sided positions, neither of which suffices. May contends that we can find the resolution of this problem in the phenomenological concept of intentionality as developed by Edmund Husserl and Martin Heidegger.

May interprets intentionality as the structure that gives meaning to experience. The root meaning of intentionality has the connotation of stretching or reaching. May plays with the etymology of the word "intend" to show the richness of the concept. The root of the word is "tend." To *tend* means to care, and May points to Heidegger's development of care as the structure of human existence. To *tend* also means to be inclined toward. The word "attend" belongs to the same family. James's idea of free will includes the ability to attend to a difficult idea. Putting these observations together, we structure our world by our *tendencies* to pay *attention* to particular possibilities. In James's example of getting out of bed in the morning, the person remained stuck as long as he paid attention to the cold floor and the warm bed. But the activities of the day, the things he cared about, became a decisive motivating force. If such care and interest were totally missing in a person's life, the pain of getting out of bed on a cold morning would be an overwhelming obstacle and the person would be caught in the grip of a crippling depression.

The question of free will must be asked again in the context of intentionality. If intentionality constitutes the structure of our world, do we choose this world, or do we at least choose within it? Can we, by effort, turn to one structure when we might have turned to another one? Are we responsible for the power of our effort? According to May, the kind of choice we can make and the amount of effort we can put into a task depends on the structure of our consciousness, that is, on intentionality. Intentionality is not limited to our cognitive understanding of the world, but also includes our entire orientation. We are capable of acting only if we see the future as a realm where action is possible. We must see possibilities and experience "I can."

William James exemplified the effectiveness of these ideas in his own life. He remained immobilized by depression until he studied and adopted Charles Renouvier's concept of will. Renouvier had defined will as "the sustaining of a thought because I choose to when I might have other thoughts" (Perry I, 323). James consented to this idea and resolved to practice it by holding the idea of freedom when he might have accepted determinism. This belief gave him the power to act freely and to overcome his depression with all of the crippling psychosomatic symptoms that went with it. Previously, the thought of being nothing but part of the chain of deterministic forces was a crushing burden. James's freedom did not result from the chance reading of Renouvier. On the contrary, his acceptance of the idea rested on his entire orientation toward such an idea. His attitude had more to do with shaping the idea than vice versa. He consented to the view, which said "I can." The future now waited with possibilities, and he enjoyed the freedom to act on them.

Freedom consists of the power to turn our attention to difficult ideas and make them effective. We in the twenty-first century may find this phrase too

Victorian, since we do not tend to see the good life as a stiff-lipped struggle of the will against bodily inclinations. Will power conjures up the specter of a *will to power* over nature and over humanity that is reflected in the major political and economic malformations of the industrial age. The notion of will power seems to have expired in the 1960s. Instead of being the center of freedom, the "will" appeared as the inhibitive power against spontaneity. As theologian Alan Watts stated: "the more consciousness is individualized by the success of the will, the more everything outside the individual seems to be a threat—including not only the external world, but also the external and uncontrolled spontaneity of one's own body."[5] From this point of view, if freedom means anything, it means a spontaneity that occurs when we are in touch with our whole self, including our bodily desires and needs, rather than a turning toward difficult ideas.

I think that it is worthwhile to rescue the idea of free will from the charges that it is one-sidedly Victorian. Our deepest wishes often take the form of ideas that we can attend to only with effort. It takes sustained effort even to pay attention to the signals of our body. As May points out, most of the time we are distracted by external noises, habits, obsessions, and defense mechanisms. We do not necessarily follow the idea, that we love and respect the most. Less valued but more immediate rival ideas tend to prevail. Without effort, things fall apart. In G. K. Chesterton's analogy, if we want a white fence, we cannot leave it alone; we must repeatedly whitewash it. The tendency for things to fall into disorder can be expected in an indeterministic universe.

If desires become disconnected from an understanding of physical reality, they become mere wishes in the pejorative sense which traditional philosophy has given to that term. James was in line with that tradition when he defined a wish as a desire for that which we believe does not lie within our power to achieve. May, however, gave *wish* a positive meaning as that which expresses our real desires and gives us motivating power. He contends that the ability to wish constitutes a condition absolutely necessary for mental health (May, 209–216). If will becomes detached from wish, or in conflict with wish, will becomes ineffective as in James's description of getting out of bed on a cold morning. The task appears to be that of integrating wish and will.

We find the meaning of free will in fulfilling those deep wishes that we believe are possible. A realistic view of freedom, as opposed to mere wishfulness, requires an understanding of the full weight of necessity that burdens every physical being. In the case of the human body, the burden includes instinct, habit, and all of the drives, compulsions, and defense mechanisms that have become part of the structure of the nervous system.

Freedom, in James's understanding does not mean *escaping* from the physical world but rather working in the world to bring about desired results.

If we are faithful in our outward actions "the world will be in so far safe and we quit of our debt to it" (WB, 174). Our duty, rather than subjective feeling, must be our master. We owe a debt to the world because the world is vulnerable. It can be hurt if we act wrongly or if we fail to do our duty. The injuries that our acts or omissions bring to the world are not inevitable, but they are possible. If the world were a totality to which no harm could come or in which no evil could be avoided, we would owe nothing to the world. The world would be self-sufficient, and our external actions would not matter. James considered the deterministic view of the world to be one that appeals only to those who seek comfort in believing that the world rests already saved and therefore free of risk, or that it lies already doomed so that we are not responsible. James rejected this attitude on grounds that he admitted could never be proved or disproved. He freely chose to be an indeterminist and acted accordingly.

Chapter 4

William James and Moral Philosophy

Although James addressed the moral issues of his time such as war, imperialism, and racism, he did not write extensively on ethical theory. He devoted only one work to that subject, the essay, "The Moral Philosopher and the Moral Life." In this essay he did not intend to show how the average person should think about moral issues, but how the moral philosopher should think about these issues. The essay investigates the question: "What should the moral philosopher do?" James did not consider philosophers to be necessarily any wiser or more ethical than anyone else and did not claim that he as a philosopher had any special insight to bring to the table. Nevertheless, the moral philosopher has a special task in helping the rest of the community create a moral universe. In describing this task, he reveals his thinking about the meaning of morality.

The Task of the Moral Philosopher

Moral philosophers go to work in an environment in which there is no ready-made moral universe. Fortunately, there are moral ideals and moral relations. The philosopher has the task of weaving the ideals and relations into a moral universe. A moral ideal is anything that anyone thinks ought to be. Ideals are given in experience before any judgment is made as to which moral ideals are better and, therefore, ought to prevail. But a multitude of moral ideals, experienced subjectively, certainly does not constitute a universe. Rather, such a situation can be termed a chaos of conflicting voices.

In setting out on his task of creating a moral universe, James distinguishes three questions: First comes *the psychological question*, which asks about the origin of these ideals. Second, the *metaphysical question* asks what the value terms mean. Finally, James asks *the casuistic question* concerning what is right in practice.

James did not devote much space to *the psychological question* in this article. He mentions the theory of associationism only to reject it. Associationism, which enjoyed much popularity in his time and provided the basis of utilitarianism, holds that we view something as good or bad because we associate it with pleasant or painful experiences in our past. James rejected associationism as incompatible with the reality of our moral experience. On the contrary he argues,

> All the more penetrating ideals are revolutionary. They present themselves far less in the guise of effects of past experience than in that of the probable causes of future experience, factors to which the environment and the lesson it has so far taught us must learn to bend. (WB, 189)

So while associationism looks backwards at the origin of preferences, morality must look ahead to how we ought to act now and in the future. As he did all through his life, James attributed an active role to thoughts. Whatever their origin, the meaning of our thoughts resides in the work that they do in shaping our world.

James attributes more importance to the *metaphysical question*: What do value terms mean? Looking at all of the claims that have been made by moral philosophers, James observes that they have only one thing in common; they all express claims. He comes to the startling conclusion that a moral ideal consists simply of satisfying a moral claim. This conclusion, at first, sounds not only startling, but also ludicrous. It seems that it either naively ignores the abundance of evil claims, or it falls into a subjectivism that cannot distinguish good from evil. To understand James, the reader must go beyond this immediate impression and carefully follow the development of his argument.

James begins with the assertion that values can exist only for conscious beings. For something to be valuable there must be someone who values it. If the world were totally dead and there were no living beings and no God, there would be no value. But if any conscious being, human or divine, or whatever other animal or other conscious being values something, it has that much value. Everything that can be called good holds a value to someone. If any conscious being expresses a value by claiming the good of something, that thing is to that extent good. Therefore, every claim ought to be satisfied unless, *and this* **unless** *is crucial,* it conflicts with another claim. To satisfy a claim is good; to frustrate a claim therefore is bad. My claim or your claim taken by itself is always good and ought to be satisfied. But if satisfying my claim frustrates you in the pursuit of your claim, then my claim, to that extent, becomes bad. To illustrate James's definition with a common example, suppose that a person valued riding a bicycle fast for exercise and fun. Taken by itself, this would be a good thing to do simply because the person values it. But if the person were to ride on a crowded sidewalk, the pedestrians' claim to safety would make the cyclist's claim bad. The *only* thing that could make his claim bad is its conflict with other claims.

A key question asks whether the conscious being values a thing because it is good or whether it is good because it is valued. Although most readers would feel more comfortable if James said that we value things because they are good, James almost certainly meant the less comforting interpretation, that they are good because of our claim. He states emphatically that the essence of good is simply to satisfy demand. (He uses the words claim and demand interchangeably.) His theory is voluntaristic, meaning that the goodness of a thing results from a will, human or divine. There is no possibility of reasoning out the good a priori. An individual might know what she considers to be good, but she cannot know what the next person considers good unless he communicates it by making his claim. Those who find this view unacceptable might offer alternatives to explain good as an objective reality that precedes anyone's claim. But James points out that there are several such candidates and that the only thing they have in common is that each of them is a claim. Further analysis of this issue will be better understood after looking at the whole theory. But for now, keep in mind that James answers the metaphysical question, "What is the meaning of good?" by affirming that the essence of good is to satisfy a claim. How to judge among conflicting claims emerges as the task of the third question.

James defines *the casuistic question* as the third question in his treatment of moral philosophy. How do we determine which claim ought to be satisfied when claims come into conflict? James offers a thought experiment to illustrate his point that every claim is good and ought to be satisfied. Imagine a hypothetical situation in which only one conscious being exists. If it made a claim, that claim should be met. The being would have an absolute right to have its claim met. Such a hypothetical world would not be a moral universe but a moral solitude in which the conscious being could determine without limit what is good and right.

But now add another conscious being so that we have a moral dualism. We can call each being's ideals right but with a limitation. When they come into conflict with each other, and both of them cannot be realized, the rightness of one would cancel that of the other. A's claim remains good in as much as it is a claim, but to the extent that it frustrates B's claim, it becomes bad. We need a standard to determine which set of ideals ought to prevail over the other. If we add as many conscious beings as we find in reality, the problem remains the same. We have a moral pluralism instead of a mere dualism, but we do not have a moral universe. Each claim, as the ideal of a conscious being, ought to be satisfied, but because the claims come into conflict, they cannot all be satisfied. Satisfying all claims presents a physical impossibility imposed by the limits of time, space, and the human life span. Reality imposes on the philosopher the task of creating a moral universe by establishing an order among the claims. James's views can be summarized by the following axioms:

> There is no preexisting order in the nature of things.
> There is no moral obligation without a claim.
> There is some obligation when there is a claim.
> Only a conflicting claim can invalidate a claim.

This group of axioms rests on the first one, that no moral order prevails in the nature of things apart from the desire, ideals, and claims of conscious beings. Things apart from conscious beings can be neither good nor bad. They become good or bad as they help or hinder conscious beings in their pursuit. If we encounter an inanimate object on which no conscious being has a claim, it imposes no obligation, passive or active. A person may pulverize a rock if no conscious being objects to the pulverization of that rock. It might be helpful to add a qualification which I believe James would approve. Saying that pulverizing the rock is permissible if no conscious being objects assumes that they would still have no objection even if everyone knew all of the results of the rock's destruction. Although this permissive attitude toward rock smashing may sound cold and harsh to rock lovers, rocks have no rights. Human beings who love rocks for aesthetic, commercial, or any other purpose, of course, may make a claim on the rock, and that claim ought to be satisfied unless it conflicts with a claim by another person.

If the essence of good is to satisfy the claims of conscious beings, what do we do when claims come into conflict with each other? How do we decide right from wrong in practice? This practical problem—James calls it the "casuistic question"—is to determine which claims ought to be satisfied and which ought to be sacrificed. We find the answer in the statement that every claim is by definition good, and it becomes bad only if it destroys the satisfaction of another claim. The highest moral ideal requires us to satisfy as many demands as possible. James states his principle for ranking conflicting claims: "Ideals are highest which prevail at the least cost, or by whose realization the least possible number of other ideals are destroyed" (WB, 205). Ordinarily this principle favors conventional morality. The ideals that have been handed down constitute an evolutionary survival as human beings learn over time how to accommodate each other. The claim that we ought to respect the person and property of others, for instance, allows more ideals to survive than anyone's claim to commit violence or theft against another.

If we ordinarily rank as the best ideals the ones tested and proven, how is moral progress made? James answers that sometimes the view held to be right may actually destroy more ideals than its rival would destroy. It takes an especially wise and courageous person to see the wrong in an accepted moral view and to act on that insight. He states as his maxim: "The highest ethical life—however few are called to bear its burdens—consists at all times in the breaking of the rules which have grown too narrow for the actual case" (WB, 209). Conventional people might judge such a person as immoral. Moral rules are developed over time to allow for a maximization of ideals. In our moral training, we learn to treat these rules as absolutes. Most of the time they can rightly be treated as absolutes and this treatment makes for social harmony and good character. But when the rules become constrictive and the person with a larger vision breaks them to make room for a better principle, that person appears to be an immoral rebel instead of a moral leader. When James was a youth, the abolitionists were considered to be wrong-minded extremists even in New England. Henry David Thoreau went to jail for refusing to pay taxes to a government that supported slavery. The rules of proper society, as well as the law, affirmed the "right" of slave owners and those who opposed the system of slave ownership seemed to be moral deviants. This is an obvious case of how the accepted morality was wrong and the opponents, who appeared to be immoral in their own time, were morally right. Many other examples of unrecognized immorality infected James's time such as oppression of former slaves after the Civil War and what John Stuart Mill called the "the subjugation of women." Examples of overcoming moral blindness in the twentieth century include the labor, civil rights, and women's movements, all of which seemed deviant in their early stages, but now take their place as part of the conventional wisdom.

The description of changes in morality evokes the question of whether there are any absolutes in morality. James affirms a nonrelative principle: "There is but one unconditional commandment, which is that we should seek incessantly, with fear and trembling, so to vote and act as to bring about the very largest total universe of good" (WB, 209). When ideals collide, the better ideal remains the one that is most inclusive. The most inclusive one does not destroy its opponent but leaves as much as possible standing. Traditional morality clearly allows for greater inclusiveness than does crime and immorality. The person who murders, for example, prevents the victim from achieving any further goals and deeply injures the ideals of the victim's friends and family. If the would-be murderer can be deterred from committing the crime, he can still have a life and choose other, less destructive desires. James's moral hero, who resists the accepted morality, also exemplifies the principle of greater inclusiveness. If those holding a majority opinion would kill, imprison, or intimidate into silence a nonconformist, they would not only frustrate the ideal which they find offensive, but they also would prevent the offender from achieving any other ideal. If the defenders of the status quo experience frustration in their desire to silence the nonconformist, they still have a life and the opportunity to achieve other goals.

It might appear at first glance that James's ethics consists of pure subjectivism. Can we really found ethics on the notion that all demands hold good unless they interfere with other demands? Further analysis will reveal that this theory does not exhibit subjectivism. The theory does not simply affirm that whatever I claim to be good is by that very fact good. It asserts rather that whatever any conscious being claims to be good is therefore good. From my point of view, your claim stands as objectively real, and according to James's theory I am morally bound to honor it. I can know the universe of claims only objectively. To be ethical means to regard my own claim as objectively as I regard your claim. Therefore the objection that James's theory constitutes mere subjectivity does not hold up. The imperative to work for the largest universe of ideals stands, according to James, as an objective and universal moral law.

The notion of more inclusive ideals holds true, not only among the several individuals who constitute groups, but also within the single individual. We as individuals can put aside some demands by simply ignoring them. Other demands will fill us with remorse and regret if they are not fulfilled. To achieve peace within oneself, a person must obey those urges that are strongest in the long run. James makes a distinction between two different moods by which individuals may be governed, the easygoing mood and the strenuous mood. The easygoing mood consists of seeking pleasure and avoiding pain. A person governed by this mood will realize a relatively small universe of ideals. Those governed by the strenuous mood forego pleasure and endure pain for the sake of larger more encompassing ideals. The strenuous mood needs "the wilder passions to arouse it, the big fears, loves, indignation or the deeply penetrating appeal of some one of the higher fidelities like justice, truth, or freedom" (WB, 211). An easygoing humanistic ethic will almost never bring out the highest moral energy. Such energy is more likely to be aroused in a person who has a religious or metaphysical belief in an infinite moral agent. The highest moral effort can be called forth when God is one of the claimants. In James's words: "Every sort of energy and endurance, of courage and capacity for handling life's evils is set free in those who have religious faith" (WB, 213). So, according to James, the role of faith in the moral life does not consist in providing rules, but rather it consists in expanding the range of ideals.

In addition to expanding the range and intensity of ideals, belief in God holds necessary if there is to be a stable moral order. The stability would not be based on a fixed code of conduct, but on the confidence that the search for moral truth proves meaningful. The postulate of God as an all-enveloping demander might help stabilize James's system, but as James admits, even if we assume that God exists and has a set of demands, we do not know what they are. A notion of what an all-knowing demander would demand could serve as an ideal. With this concept, we could assert that a moral truth prevails. The moral truth consists of the sum of all claims that we would make if we strove to satisfy as many claims as possible, if we knew what all of the claims were, and if we could determine the best way to satisfy them.

James defines the task of the moral philosopher as the creation of the moral universe, a moral republic that satisfies as many demands as possible. In this role, he did not wish to be a partisan to any particular set of demands. Outside of this role he did assert some claims as to what ranks as good and what does not. The next step in our investigation will be to present James's own ideals, and to show whether they achieve compatibility with his idea of the moral universe. The final question will be to see whether the ideals that James espoused are the only ideals compatible with the moral universe.

James's Moral Ideals

Gerald Myers identifies James's personal morality as a morality of optimism. He uses the term in a very general sense to include what James called "meliorism." James rejected pessimism because it holds that no betterment is possible. But he also rejected optimism which teaches that no betterment is possible or even desirable. If optimism means that this world ranks as the best of all possible worlds, then, by definition, the world can not become better. James argued that materialism necessarily implies pessimism, meaning that the salvation of our ideals is impossible, while the belief in the Absolute exhibits optimism, meaning that the salvation of our ideals rests assured. James called his own position "meliorism," the belief that salvation, while possible, cannot be guaranteed, and that our effort can make things better.

Meliorism leads its adherents to believe that the individual can be effective and to act on that belief. James illustrated the power of meliorism in his own life. As described in chapter 3, James's personal psychological problem of depression was resolved when he found through Renouvier that he could believe that his will is free. This belief was expressed in his essay, "Is Life Worth Living" in which he showed that the suicidal outlook can be overcome by a religious or metaphysical view that makes effective action possible. If every event, including thought, is physically determined, human action reflects an illusion. Effective human action holds possible only in an indeterministic universe. Further, such action remains impossible if the salvation of the world has already been achieved by an Absolute Being and our world of struggles expresses only an illusion. We can act meaningfully only in a world which stands in need for salvation and in which salvation is possible but still a work in progress. James held that theism makes human action possible in that we and God work together in a hopeful struggle to make salvation an actuality.

If we humans can affect the world by our actions, we need to find a basis for what constitutes affecting the world in a beneficial way, and not merely affecting it. James believed that our worldview, our philosophy, determines what kind of actions we will perform. In "Reflex Action and Theism," he argues that the belief most compatible with the human mind, hence most rational, is theism. The theistic view, provided that it is not a superstitious or fundamentalist interpretation, is compatible with reason, with the facts of science, and most importantly with the active willing nature of the human person.

There are many interpretations of theism. Can the compatibility with reason be met by a national or tribal war god? James clearly rejects this conclusion; but what was the basis of his rejection? The answer to this question seems to lie in the awareness of the truth that every individual represents a life that is worth living. James makes this point clear in his essay, "On a Certain Blindness in Human Beings." The blindness consists in looking at other people externally so as to miss their inner drama and joy. As an example, he cites his first impression of the settlers in the mountains of North Carolina who cleared patches in the woods to create their small farms. From an outsider's view, it looked like nothing more than the ugly scarring of a once beautiful landscape. But the full meaning of the farmers' effort opened up to James when one of the farmers told him: "We are never satisfied unless we are bringing one of these under cultivation."[1] James then realized that the clearing expressed the drama of one family's triumph over the elements. He finds another example of the often-missed truth of an individual's life in the young man who loves a young woman who appears homely to outsiders. Jack sees beauty in his Jill, not because love is blind, but because love is clear-sighted. Those who miss the beauty in Jill miss the joy and therefore miss everything. The beauty, the joy, and the drama that lie hidden in people reveal the dimension of reality that transcends the world of ordinary perceptions. Yet, once the blindness is overcome, this dimension shows up in what had been seen as commonplace. The overcoming of blindness reveals that any oppressive political structure can be condemned as false and immoral.[2]

James demonstrated his own moral commitment by the public positions that took on the controversial issues of his time. These issues included the situation of Blacks, women, and immigrants. He denounced the imperialism of the Spanish American War and the annexation of the Philippines. He took strong stands on medical and educational issues and on the mistreatment of animals in vivisection. He held it as a duty to intervene whenever justice and the respect for the individual failed (Myers, 422, 429). Each act of injustice and disrespect reflects the blindness of bad worldviews that miss the inner reality of other persons.

The moral imperative, which requires us to try to see the meaning in another person's life, impels each of us to make our own life significant. James does not express this obligation in the language of imperatives, but the conclusion that the reader arrives at in seeing what James means by a *significant life*, is that we should each try to live such a life. In his essay, "What Makes a Life Significant?" James compares the pleasant but easy life of the intellectuals at a summer Chautauqua camp to the life of the laborers facing hardship and danger day after day. The privileged intellectual and the hard-pressed laborer might each be living meaningless lives, although the opportunity for meaning was available to each of them. The Chautauqua life lacked risk, danger, hardship, and challenge. The laborers, by contrast, had all of these elements, but their lives could still be insignificant if they remain unaware of the ideal dimension of their own struggle. James concluded that a significant life has two requirements. These requirements were strenuousness and ideal novelty.

James confirmed his preference for the strenuous life by an appeal to intuition. We can simply see that a life of ease is not significant. We naturally admire the person who has achieved something against odds, with great effort or danger, and shedding blood, sweat, and tears. This appeal seems to be aesthetic but it can also be justified on ethical grounds. If good comes easily, it does not constitute much change from the existing order. In James's view, for an action to be good, it must make a difference. He did not mean that every difference is good. But in a world that is deficient and in which individuals are vulnerable, any change that enhances the opportunity of individuals to be significant is to that extent good. Mere struggle of labor that does not make a difference—that does not change anything—is not meaningful. James rejects the "oriental fatalism" that he sees in Tolstoy's glorification of the peasant who simply accepts his plight. The only thing that could make a strenuous life bad is if it hindered or destroyed the opportunity for other persons to live meaningful lives. We can find the meaning of life in the struggle against the deficiencies of reality as it happens to be.

In addition to strenuousness, James requires ideality. An ideal overcomes the deadness and repetitiveness of matter. The necessary characteristics of an ideal are consciousness and novelty. The novelty need not be absolute as long as it is new to the conscious actor. What may be commonplace to one person may be a triumph of spirit for another. For example, one person can go through life without having to struggle against the temptation of drunkenness. For another person, sobriety ranks not only as a hard-earned achievement, but as a new and exciting experience. Since reality as we find it needs redemption, a meaningful life must involve an ideal awareness of how reality ought to be made anew, and the willingness to act strenuously for the renewal.

James's ethics may be summed up by the concept of "the religion of democracy." He used this term to connote that by overcoming our ancestral blindness to the inner life of every person, no matter how insignificant they may be or appear to be, we are getting in touch with the highest reality. Although James rejected a monistic notion of an Absolute, he believed in a higher and hidden unity that finds expression in the ideal of the moral universe. The harmony that constitutes a moral universe will not be perfect, and some things will be lost. But the harmony of our world is partly real and partly a possibility. We have as our moral task to bring as much of the possibility into reality as we can. People can fulfill their moral task in whatever sphere they work; science, art, religion, education, labor, business, politics. The moral imperative reflects all of James's theory and practice.

The Adequacy of James's Theory

Even a very careful study leaves the reader, at least this reader, wondering about the adequacy of James's theory. The reader may find it is hard to deal with a theory of ethics founded on the claims of those whose conduct it is supposed to guide. We may yearn for an objective criterion that stands outside of anyone's subjective needs and wants. The fact that James contended that morality requires that we value everyone's claims and not just our own is probably not enough to assuage the fear that his theory consists of subjective relativism. The theory has only limited pedagogical value since it is more likely than not to be misunderstood. However, when properly understood, James's theory can deeply enrich our understanding of the moral life. He based his theory on the reality of the inner life. In our materialistic worldview, only external things are considered real. We use the dismissive adverb "merely" when we describe the activity of the inner life as in the phrases "merely subjective" or "merely psychological." Even some religious persons who claim to believe in a soul are put off by the notion of the inner life being a basis for the knowledge of good and evil. James struggled to provide a theory that not only acknowledges the reality of the inner life of persons, but also makes it the basis for determining the good life.

Chapter 5

Rationality and Religious Faith

The question of religious faith permeates much of James's writing. He saw the possibility of living a meaningful life threatened on two sides, materialism and absolutism. Materialism presented the world as a dead and meaningless machine in which nothing that we cared about mattered. In the late nineteenth century, among English-speaking philosophers, the only serious rival to materialism was the belief in the Absolute. This had been developed by several English idealists, notably F. H. Bradley, and was a direct descendent of G. W. F. Hegel and German idealism. James rejected the notion of the Absolute as a "metaphysical monster" who would leave no room for human agency. Idealism leads to an optimistic outlook unlike the pessimistic view of materialism, but neither leave room for human agency. James found both of these views to be crushingly depressing. He suggested instead, a pragmatic interpretation of the religious hypothesis. He interprets the salvation of the world as *possible*. His view opposes the materialists who deny the possibility of salvation and also opposes the absolute idealists who believe salvation is guaranteed. James considered the pragmatic interpretation of belief in salvation to be the most rational approach.

To understand James's view of the rationality of religious belief, we must recall his general notion of the three functions of the human mind: perception, thinking, and action. In contemporary jargon we could call these functions "input, process, and output." The task of thinking is to interpret the information from the senses so that meaningful action is possible. As explained in chapter 1, an interpretation that we are prepared to act on is a *belief*. Anything offered as a possible object of belief is an hypothesis. In analyzing the role of the mind in religious belief, James defined the object of religious belief as "the religious hypothesis." James judged every hypothesis by the pragmatic test. What difference will it make to anyone if this hypothesis is true? This question reveals the meaning of the hypothesis so that we can make a judgment about its truth value. What is the pragmatic meaning of the religious hypothesis? In his essay, "The Will to Believe," James asserts the religious hypothesis consists of the two most essential affirmations of religion. First, "The best things are the more eternal things," and second, "we are better off even now if we believe her (religion's) first affirmation to be true" (WB, 25). This proposition runs contrary to the materialist belief that there can be no eternal things and that belief in them constitutes an illusory and self-defeating belief in "pie in the sky." James poses the pragmatic question of whether the world can be saved and what we human beings can and should do about it.

Faith in the Salvation of the World

James does not define what the salvation of the world means, and he believed that each person has the right to have some say in what it means. Each of us has some ideals whose survival and prosperity have crucial importance for us. We experience some agreement among ourselves although not total agreement. Nearly all of us would consider the salvation of the world to be incompatible with the utter destruction of ourselves, our loved ones, our work, and our progeny. Yet, we must expect total destruction if the materialist hypothesis holds true. So if materialists think about the salvation of the world at all, they must do so as pessimists. There is no hope.

The believers in the Absolute, as James understands them, see the salvation of the world as guaranteed. There is no chance of failure. James contended that this view provides comfort to some, and it enables them to take a moral vacation, in fact to be on a permanent vacation, because the Absolute will take care of everything. James finds the idea of the Absolute unacceptable because it does not give us anything to do. We sit as spectators rather than players in the contest whose victory rests assured without us. (I should mention that Josiah Royce, who believed in the Absolute, emphatically denied that it gave us a "moral holiday" and reduced us to spectators. James contrasted his view of the possibility of salvation with a particular interpretation of the Absolute.)

James offers a third alternative that presents the salvation of the world as neither impossible nor necessary. Salvation looms as a real *possibility* that *may or may not* be achieved. The world is neither a product of mechanistic determinism nor of divine predestination. James believed in an undetermined universe, a place where chance events occur, where both risk and opportunity abound, and where human beings can make things happen that might not happen.

To call an event possible means first that it is neither impossible, nor actual, nor necessarily going to become actual. To say x is possible means that it does not exist, but it can come to exist or it might not. Minimal conditions for x to be possible are freedom from self-contradiction, and from the influence of anything that would interfere with its actualization. These minimal conditions constitute bare possibility. However, a possibility may be positively grounded in the presence of some of the conditions for its actualization. As more of these conditions are brought forward, the possibility becomes further grounded until it becomes an actuality.

To apply the concept of increasing possibility to the salvation of the world, each of us has an idea of what it would mean to affirm the salvation of the world. Assume that you have an idea of the salvation of the world that is not intrinsically impossible. Your own ideals are part of it. You and other people who share the ideals compose part of the positive grounding of the possibility. Your ability and willingness to act on the ideal, ground it further. Your action helps to cause that part of the actualization for which you bear responsibility. If enough people who share these ideals act effectively, and if they do not succumb to stronger forces acting against them, then the ideal will be to that extent actualized. James believed in the possibility of the salvation of the world on a piece by piece basis rather than all-or-nothing; risk and loss happen.

So far, this description sounds like a humanistic moral striving with no reference to religion. However, although James denied the Absolute, he affirmed the rationality of belief in God, and held that his ideas about the possibility of salvation fit more closely to historical religion than does the philosophical concept of the Absolute. Religion expresses a real struggle between good and evil with pain, risk, and loss. James understood God to be an ally who shared some of our ideals and would struggle along with us to realize them. In this view, the game is still being played, the matter is not settled. God does all He can. We need to work with all of our might to do our part, and our part makes a difference. This idea answers the pragmatic question; "What difference does it make in anyone's life if God exists?" If James interprets reality correctly and both the materialists and the Absolute idealists miss the mark, then the salvation of the world stands possible but not guaranteed, and a tremendous burden rests on each of us.

In the essay, "Reflex Action and Theism," James presents the belief in God as the most rational belief for the human mind. He does not, here, argue for the existence of God. The existence of God could be concluded by affirming the premise that the most rational view is true. We can frame James' argument as a *modus ponens* argument that if the most rational belief is true, then the theistic view is true. But James did not attempt to prove that the most rational view is true and any such argument would be question begging. Proving that the theistic view is the most rational presents enough of a burden.

In stipulating what he meant by the theistic view, James noted that the word "God" has been employed to denote many beliefs for which writers wished to give honorific connotations, for example, the laws of nature. But James asserts that whatever else a theistic belief may entail, it essentially holds that God is the highest power in the universe and a mental personality distinct from ours. Whatever ways the human and divine personalities would resemble or differ from each other, they would be alike in that "both have purposes for which they deeply care, and each can hear the other's call" (WB, 122). James does not defend an abstraction or some vague force as the object of religious faith, but rather a personal God.

The Meaning of Rationality

When he presents his view of theism as the most rational for the human mind James presupposes a reflex-action model of the human mind. As stated at the beginning of this chapter, James held that the mind has three functions: perception, thought, and action. Perception consists of receiving impressions from the senses. Every impression will necessarily lead to some outgoing action or reaction of the muscles, the glands or both. The middle term consists of our ability to think, that is, to form concepts and to reflect on the sensations and the possible actions to take in response to the sensations. The distinguishing characteristic of James's thought, that which distinguished him from much of the philosophical tradition, consists of the belief that thoughts have no meaning other than the possible actions to which they may lead. The whole thinking process takes place in the middle term of a reflex arc, which remains incomplete until it finds consummation in some action.

The controversial nature of this theory calls for a brief digression to explain why James held this belief. It can partly be explained by his work on the physiology of the nervous system and the knowledge of the fact that all of the neural pathways work as either "afferent," carrying impulses to the brain, or "efferent," sending messages to the muscles for appropriate response to the incoming sensations. The brain, in a human or an animal, determines the appropriate action as when the sensations show the possibility of eating or being eaten. James's fascination with the physiological conditions of thinking could have led in several directions. For example, it could have led to a reductive materialism; thought is nothing but the result of the central nervous system sorting out the afferent and efferent impulses for the survival of the organism. On the other hand, a person with a philosophical temperament might conclude that no matter how the thought process evolved, now that we have it, it stands out as the most excellent of human faculties and deserves to be esteemed for its own sake. The latter view would affirm Aristotle's contention that human happiness consists in the unimpeded exercise of speculative reason.

James was a physiologist with a philosophical temperament, but he rejected both of the above options as irrational. He found in his own life that theoretical speculation does not lead to ecstasy, or happiness, or even contentment. Rather, it can lead to despair and thoughts of suicide. Theory can be distressing because when we push speculation far enough we hit a wall. We encounter what today we call the "existential question." "Why is there anything at all instead of nothing?" Here the mind is stopped. The flow is dammed up and has no place to go. Through this experience of despair James found the solution that became his life-guiding principle, that thought flows meaningfully if and only if it leads to action. Even if our speculative mind gets stopped up, the world is rational as long as we can act. When we convert our thoughts into action, the flow continues. We affirm rationality in practice. A rational view makes action possible and thereby continues the flow of thought. This insight supports the belief in the pragmatic theory of meaning and the reflex arc theory of mind. Theorizing for its own sake leads to an intellectual, emotional, and spiritual dead-end; theorizing for the sake of action can release the flow of thought in the service of meaningful action.

After this digression on why James contended that the role of thinking is to serve action, we are in position to understand what James means by a rational belief. He sees a rational belief as one that leads to action. Any interpretation of the universe, to be considered rational, must do justice to the facts of experience, the demand of the mind for consistency, and the needs of the practical volitional nature to act. Shortchanging any one of these renders the view irrational. We will now examine the meaning of rationality in each of the three aspects of the mind.

The world as given to the senses lacks rationality and it calls for no line of action. The given reality consists of a chaos that would overwhelm our mind with the immensity of available sensations. "The real world as it is given objectively at this moment is the sum of all of its beings and events now. But can we think of such a sum?"(WB, 118–119). The real order of the world stands as a collective contemporaneity consisting of an infinite number of relations. James points out that we cannot handle this order and "we have nothing to do with it except get away from it as fast as possible" (WB, 119). We do this by organizing it into history, art, science, and other human constructs. It is only by means of these constructs that we can feel at home.

Of the infinite relations out of which we construct our familiar worlds, some, such as contiguity are given to our senses, while others such as mathematical relations are not. We choose which of the relations we consider essential and ignore the rest. But those relations that we consider essential are essential only to our purposes. The others that we ignore are just as real. The mind carves out a human world from the infinity of real events and relations. It does this to serve the volitional nature that requires simple concepts and foresight to act. But while the mind chooses an actual human world from an infinity of possibilities, it must choose from what reality gives. It cannot make up events and relations just to fulfill its purposes, neither can it deny or ignore real events and relations that might thwart its purposes. To do so would be irrational.

While the first function of the mind receives the facts of experience, the second function forms concepts for a teleological purpose, and the third function, the volitional, imposes its demands on the theorizing function. James anticipated an objection that the volitional function has no right to impose its demands on thought. Rather, thought should be based on what is given. James answers that without teleology, the mind would have no concepts at all. It could not choose from the infinite relations given in the senses and would experience only the "big buzzing, blooming confusion." The whole conceptualizing function of the mind serves to show us the way from the state of things that the senses reveal to the state of things that the will desires. To be rational, a worldview must not only be in conformity to the appropriate facts of experience, but also must have the internal consistency and submission to the rules of thought that will enable it to successfully lead from the perceived to the desired reality.

A rational worldview must lead to meaningful action, which constitutes the purpose of the whole process. If a worldview leads to a "wall," as James said of pure theory, or if it leads nowhere as with idle thoughts and disputes, it is not rational. If the worldview gives us a picture of reality in which nothing seems worth doing; if we ask "Is life worth living?" and come up empty, the view is not rational. A rational view must not only present the possibility of action, but it must appeal to our passions strongly enough to evoke action.

The Reasonableness of Theism

With this description of what James meant by rationality, we can begin to understand his thesis: "God, whether existent or not, is the kind of being which, if he did exist, would form the most adequate possible object for minds framed like our own to conceive as lying at the root of the universe"(WB, 115). If James's thesis is correct, it does not show whether or not God exists. But it shows that belief in God stands as the most rational of beliefs. Unanswered questions surround the issue of whether the most rational of beliefs is true. Is the universe rational? Is there a co-naturality between the universe and the deepest needs of the rational mind? But the task at hand requires an examination of James' argument that the theistic belief stands as the most rational.

The discussion of the reflex theory of the mind shows that a rational belief would be one that enables the thinker to choose, from the possible worlds compatible with experience, an internally consistent world that empowers action to produce desired results in the world of experience. A simplistic theism, for example, one based on a literal interpretation of the Bible, would not work because it does not conform to our scientific understanding of the universe. James calls such a view idolatrous and points out that the experiencing function of the mind, department number one, comes in "with its battery of facts and dislodges her from her dogmatic repose" (WB, 128). On the other hand, if the mind accepts the facts of experience in their mere mechanical outwardness, the volitional function of the mind will find itself in a world that refuses hospitality to its needs. To quote James on the role which theism can play, he said:

> Now theism always stands ready with the most practically rational solution it is possible to conceive. Not an energy of our active nature, to which it does not authoritatively appeal, not an emotion of which it does not normally and naturally release the springs. At a simple stroke it changes the dead blank *it* of the world into a living *thou* with whom the whole man may have dealings. (WB, 127)

If a theistic view is sophisticated enough to be in conformity with the known facts of science, and to be internally consistent, its energizing effect on our practical nature makes it more rational than any materialist worldview. James had argued the same point more forcefully in his essay on moral philosophy, "The Moral Philosopher and the Moral Life" as discussed in the previous chapter. But before developing this idea further, it is important to answer the objection that this view merely reflects wishful thinking. Are we justified in proposing a false view as long as it inspires us? The answer, of course, is no, and James would not propose such a thing. He joked about the child in Sunday school who defined faith as "believing something which you know ain't true." Nevertheless, James did affirm the right to believe in cases of forced and momentous options that cannot be resolved by our intellectual nature.

In the essay under discussion, "Reflex Action and Theism," James had shown that the human mind forms a world from the infinite possibilities given in immediate sense experience. The world as we form it serves our volitional nature. As James says, "The conceiving or theorizing faculty—the mind's middle compartment—functions exclusively for the sake of ends that do not exist at all in the world of impressions we receive from our senses, but are set by our emotional and practical subjectivity altogether" (WB, 117). We take a given state of affairs and try to remake it into a state of affairs demanded by our volitional nature. But in what he calls "the miracle of miracles," the given order bends, at least somewhat to our desires and our efforts to remodel it. The scientist, the artist, and the person of practical affairs share the belief that the world will respond to their action if it is the right action. If they fail, they try again. They assume that "the impressions of sense must give way, must be reduced to the desiderated form. They all postulate in the interest of their volitional nature a harmony between the latter and the nature of things. The theologian does no more" (WB, 120). Religious thought has the same intent and the same outcome as all other reasonable human pursuits. If we must consider religious thought irrational because it molds the given perceptions into a world where human action becomes meaningful, then we must also judge all of the other human endeavors as irrational. James argues that none of these activities is inherently irrational although a person pursuing any one of them might be irrational, for example, scientists or business leaders who reject or ignore relevant information because it does not fit their own self-serving ideas. We find the very meaning of rationality precisely in the act of fashioning a meaningful world out of the chaos of impressions.

Does all of this give any reason to believe that God does exist or does it merely show that it would be desirable if he did? James does not try to answer this because he held that the question of whether or not God exists cannot be answered by our intellectual nature. He rejects the dogmatic position of those who say that we must be agnostics, and contends that we may be agnostics, atheists, or believers. The essential difference between belief and unbelief hinges on whether we believe that the world provides a congenial home to the rational mind. In the context of arguing for belief in God as the most rational for the human mind, he said,

> Whether over and above this He be really the living truth is another question. If He is, it will show the structure of the mind to be in accordance with the nature of reality. Whether it be or not in such accordance is, it seems to me, one of the questions that belongs to the province of personal faith to decide. (WB, 116)

Whether we believe, doubt, or reject the idea of a harmony between our faculty and the truth, we are responsible for our decision and for risks and benefits that result from it.

William James's Personal Faith

William James wrote much about the reasonableness of faith without tipping his own hand. As one writer said, he defended the right to believe but there is a question as to how much he himself exercised that right. We find one place in which he affirms a personal belief in the "Conclusions" to the *Varieties of Religious Experience*.[1] In these Gifford Lectures of 1901 and 1902, he treated such topics as conversion, saintliness, mysticism, and others as a sympathetic but detached observer. He concludes that in spite of different theologies that appear incompatible, all of the world religions demonstrate a common core of beliefs and psychological characteristics. Religious life includes the following beliefs:

1. That the visible world is part of a more spiritual universe from which it draws its chief significance;
2. That union or harmonious relation with that higher universe is our true end;
3. That prayer or inner communion with the spirit thereof—be that Spirit God or Law—is a process wherein work is really done, and spiritual energy flows in and produces effects, psychological or material, within the phenomenal world.
   Religion also includes the following psychological characteristics:—
4. A new zest which adds itself like a gift to life, and takes the form either of lyrical enchantment or of appeal to earnestness and heroism.
5. An assurance of safety and a temper of peace, and, in relation to others, a predominance of loving affections. (VRE, 367)

James examines these beliefs and characteristics and concludes that, far from being an anachronistic survival from prescientific times, religion takes its place among the most important biological activities of human beings. This conclusion exonerates the meaning and value of religious beliefs, but still leaves open the question of whether they hold true.

After indicating that religious faith can be vindicated on subjective factors, James moves the question to the objective content of religion. He asks whether in spite of discrepancies in belief among religions, there is a "common nucleus" to which they all bear witness. His answer is affirmative and that it consists of two parts:

1. An uneasiness; and
2. Its solution.

1. The uneasiness reduced to its simplest terms is a sense that there is *something wrong about us* as we naturally stand.
2. The solution is the sense that *we are saved from the wrongness*, by making connection with the higher powers. (VRE, 383)

James offers both a psychological interpretation and an "over-belief." His psychological explanation avoids reductionism, that is, he does not say that religion is "nothing but" a psychological phenomenon. Instead he tries to bolster the credibility of faith claims by showing their continuity with our scientific understanding of psychology. By over-belief, he means systematic interpretations that individuals or cultures give to faith experiences. For example, a Christian and a Hindu may have a mystical experience in which their feelings have much in common.[2] The attitude and practice of each will also have much in common especially an enhancement of the attitude of love and service. The stories and theologies of Christianity and Hinduism provide examples of over-beliefs. James considered the over-beliefs to be very important since they constitute the beliefs that guide the actions of the believers. For this reason they should be held in reverence unless they themselves express intolerance toward other beliefs.[3]

James's psychological explanation rests on an affirmation of a *subconscious self*, which in James's words "is nowadays a well-accredited psychological entity" (VRE, 386). In earlier chapters, James had described experiences such as the unification of the divided soul, conversion, and mysticism, in which something new comes into consciousness, something that clearly comes from outside yet feels very familiar, and easily becomes one's own. Since these experiences do not belong to ordinary waking conscious, they appear to come from outside, yet they are continuous with consciousness, and so enjoy familiarity.

James did not reduce the subconscious to an individual mechanism as Freud did. Rather, James saw the extension of our conscious life into a subconscious life as "something more," something that expanded the life of those who came in contact with it and something that had real effects on the persons and their practical life. James ventured into his own over-belief to posit that the "something more" is at once the extension of the human self and also a transpersonal reality that Christians and others refer to as God. James distils what he finds common to all religions in spite of various over-beliefs:

> ...we have in *the fact that the conscious person is continuous with a wider self through which saving experiences come*, a positive content of religious experience which, it seems to me, *is literally and objectively true as far as it goes*. (VRE, 388) (Emphasis in original).

To go further, we have to employ over-beliefs.

In offering his own over-belief, James suggests that the further limits of our being plunge us into a dimension other than and different from the famil-iar world of sense and understanding. It constitutes the dimension that some call the mystical or supernatural. Since our ideal impulses originate in the transpersonal dimension, and since nothing feels more intimate to us than our ideals, we belong to the transpersonal ideal realm more intimately than we belong to the visible world. Far from considering this realm to be merely imaginary, James affirms its reality.

> Yet the unseen region in question is not merely ideal, for it produces effects in this world. When we commune with it, work is actually done upon our finite personality, for we are turned into new men, and consequences in the way of conduct follow in the natural world upon our regenerative change. (VRE, 389)

James observes that "for us Christians" the higher part of the universe is called God, and we and God have business with each other. In the very last page of *Varieties*, James comes as close, I believe, as he ever did to making a personal faith statement.

> What the more characteristically divine facts are, apart from the actual flow of energy in the faith-state and the prayer-state, I know not. But the over-belief on which I am ready to make my personal venture is that they exist. (VRE, 393)

James admits that he can put himself into what he calls the "sectarian scien-tist's" attitude and imagine that the only reality is that of sensations and sci-entific laws. But he cannot really believe that reality is so limited. The openness to a "higher" region does not inhibit his ability to do science, but it represents a realm in which science, religions, and everything in between make sense, and real action is possible.

Human Immortality

The question of human immortality generally goes hand in hand with the question of the reality of God. In James's discussion of salvation, he dealt with salvation of the world rather than salvation of individual souls. Salvation of the world meant that our best ideals would survive the destruc-tion of the material world. While the emphasis on the world rather than the self shows greater generosity than does the yearning for personal salvation, James had said elsewhere that we experience nothing as more real than the pinch of our own destiny. Therefore we need to ask whether our destiny includes immortality.

James omnivorous interest in learning included an interest in the paranormal. The death of his infant son and his wife's firm belief in survival heightened his interest in the question of immortality.[4] When his friend, Frederick Myers, author of *Human Personality and its Survival after Death*, lay dying, James waited outside his door with a notebook at hand. He had promised his friend that he would record any communication that his departing soul might send. But he received no message (Simon, 297–8). James's making and keeping the promise shows that he did not consider it frivolous. When asked by a correspondent about his belief in immortality, he replied that it was "never keen." However, his friend and biographer, Ralph Barton Perry stated flatly, "... but as James grew older he came to *believe* in immortality" (Perry II, 356). Perry explains that James was motivated by practical needs. In explaining why he was only coming to this belief in 1904, at the age of sixty-two he answered, "Because I am just getting fit to live" (Perry II, 356).

In his Ingersoll lectures, "On Human Immortality," James argued against the materialists who saw such a belief as hopelessly irrational. He did not try to prove the fact of immortality since he saw the issue as one that could not be proved or disproved on strictly intellectual grounds. But he showed how immortality could be possible, with the intent of dislodging what seems to be a clinching argument against it. The argument against immortality stands clear and easy to understand. The materialists argue that, since all consciousness including feeling, thought, memory, and personal identity depends on the brain, when the brain undergoes destruction, these functions cannot exist. This conclusion finds support in the common experience that accident, disease, intoxication, or anesthetics can impair and even totally shut down the functions of consciousness. How can we believe that the complete destruction of the brain at death would lead to anything other that the complete annihilation of consciousness?

James changes the terms of the argument by pointing out that although the brain is necessary for an individual's thought, it need not be considered as the *source* of the thought. Instead, the function of the brain might be transmissive, compared to a prism, which transmits but does not produce light, or the permissive function of the trigger of a crossbow, which releases but does not produce the propellant force of the arrow. In setting the boundaries of his argument James says:

> My thesis now is this: that when we think of the law that thought is a function of the brain, we are not required to think of productive function only; *we are entitled to consider permissive or transmissive function*. And this the ordinary psychologist leaves out of his account.[5] (Italics in original).

According to the transmissive theory, thought is real and independent of any brain. But specially organized matter such as a brain has the capacity to pick up thought. The physical limitations of the brain limit and modify the thought. James uses the analogy of a threshold that is lowered in the human brain when awake, and can be made even lower in times of heightened lucidity. This theory seems to be most compatible with the notion of a world soul. According to this interpretation, the world soul is filtered through each human organism creating a sense of individuality. If the transmission theory is true and the source of consciousness survives our bodily death, it leaves open the question of how much, if anything, of our individuality survives. James recommends such question to future researchers. He stipulated that he did not intend to write a general work on immortality, but only to show that immortality can be compatible with the brain-function theory of our earth consciousness.

James addresses the question of whether the simpler productive theory of the materialist is more scientific. Certainly, the condition of the brain can increase or decrease the function of consciousness—with contemporary brain imaging this can be done more precisely than in James's time. But the only relation that a science can note between thought and brain activity is one of concomitant variation. To claim that the brain produces the thought is no more scientific than to say that the brain transmits the thought. Thought and brain are very different from each other and every theory of their relationship looks like the explanation of a miracle. The function of James's lecture was "permissive." He showed his audience that they may, without sacrificing scientific and philosophical integrity, believe in immortality.

In his treatment of religious themes; God, salvation of the world, and human immortality, James showed that belief in these ideas was at least as rational as the attitude of the agnostic and atheist. The next and final chapter on James, will be an interpretation of the practical aspects of James's religious thought. What kind of personal life or spirituality can flow from this stream of James's thought?

Chapter 6

Human Nature and the Life of the Spirit

hile the previous chapter dealt with James's understanding of religious belief, the current chapter explores the practical meaning of religious belief that can be derived from his writings. The development of the inner life is generally called "spirituality" although this should not be confused with "spiritualism"—getting in touch with ghosts. James had a lively interest in the latter, but this interest does not constitute the subject of this chapter. The term spirituality has always been familiar to religious people and today it also finds favor among those who are interested in inner development but who find the term "religion" too weighted down with ecclesiastical connotations. In James's own study of religion he dealt only with inner meanings and avoided institutional manifestations altogether. In *The Varieties of Religious Experience,* he distinguished "personal religion" from theology and from churches and argued that personal religion holds the more essential position; theology and ecclesiastical institutions remain secondary. He stipulated that his own study would be limited to personal religion. He said of the way he circumscribed his topic,

> Religion, therefore, as I now ask you arbitrarily to take it, shall mean for us, *the feelings acts and experiences of individual men in their solitude, so far as they apprehend themselves to stand in relation to whatever they consider divine.* (VRE, 42) (Italics in original).

For what James called "personal religion" I will use the term "spirituality," without prejudice one way or the other toward the value of institutional religion. This chapter will proceed by first attempting to define "spirituality" and then examining James's comments on the things defined as spiritual, whether he explicitly calls them spiritual or not.

Spirituality Defined and Placed in a Metaphysical Context

In attempting to define spirituality, I will stipulate that its essential characteristics are consciousness, freedom, and community. Spirituality must first of all be a conscious activity rather than a static substance. A non-active spirit is unthinkable. The most common metaphor, and the etymological basis for spirit, is "breath." A non-active spirit would be like a breath that does not breathe. Spirituality also connotes consciousness. At the very minimum it must be at the level of ordinary human consciousness, and the term usually implies quite a bit more. Second, spiritual activity must be not only conscious, but also must have a degree of freedom that overcomes any kind of determinism; biological, psychological, or cultural. Spirituality involves freedom in the sense of conscious self-direction. Third, spirit is communal and does not have the non-penetrability of physical matter. Two spiritual beings do not meet like billiard balls, but rather, interpenetrate each other. Spiritual beings can become real communities and not mere aggregates.

The most essential meaning of spirituality consists of freedom from the past. Spirituality implies the ability to change. The first directive of any spiritual leader states: "Reform your life." As James showed in *The Varieties of Religious Experience,* every religion presents something wrong with our life as we happen to be and it offers a way of deliverance (VRE, 383). This characteristic applies to spirituality whether it is explicitly religious or not. The development of spirituality presupposes the belief that our life as we find it is not all that it can be and that we have the possibility for something qualitatively better. The possibility of becoming better by turning our life into something qualitatively different than it happens to be provides a necessary condition for anything that we would ever call spiritual. Spirituality, therefore, requires a metaphysics that allows for a possibility for real change.

The key metaphysical presupposition for spirituality asserts that there are real possibles. Possibles, as described in chapter 5 in the context of the world's salvation, constitute a third realm between being and nonbeing. To call something possible means that it is neither actual, necessary, nor impossible. Human spirituality implies that the past does not wholly determine the future and that there is nothing that can prevent us from becoming something more than what we happen to be, or what we would become if we simply stayed on the course that we currently follow. Spirituality also implies something in us or outside of us that grounds the possibility and makes it more probable.

While the affirmation of real possibilities constitutes a necessary condition for spirituality, it is not sufficient. Human possibilities could be conceived of as limited to material possibilities such as greater wealth, an increase in physical strength, more exquisite beauty, better technology, and longevity. So the question concerns what constitutes a spiritual possibility. The question must be answered in the context of continuity rather than a sharp dichotomy. James's descriptions of mystical experience in "Mysticism," Lectures XVI and XVII of *The Varieties of Religious Experience*, provide more specific examples of the general idea of "spirituality" used here (VRE, 292–293). As James defines mysticism, its qualities include: "ineffability" meaning that the experience transcends language; having a "noetic quality" which makes the experience authoritative to those who have the experience; "transience" in that no one can sustain the experience continuously; and "passivity" in the receptivity of the experience. (The experience can turn the person into being extraordinarily active as in the case of most religious founders and leaders.) James details the various forms of spiritual experience in his lectures on "Mysticism." We find the "simplest rudiment" of such experiences in the deepened sense of a word or a phrase. The most developed form in all religions consists of a sense of union with or immersion in the ultimate reality. All levels of the mystical experience have in common a sense that ordinary personal boundaries disappear and the person becomes united with something larger. So rather than seeing experiences as spiritual or non-spiritual, we can speak of them as being more or less spiritual.

The question of what constitutes spirituality can be answered by imagining the poles of a spectrum. What would a totally non-spiritual being be like? We can think of a particle of Newtonian matter; dead, inert, moved and determined only by external forces, and impenetrable. We understand a pure spirit, by contrast, as conscious, self-determined, and able to enter communion with other spiritual beings. We humans are obviously not pure spirits and we have much of Newtonian inertness about us. But if we have a degree of self-awareness, self-determination, and openness to community, then to that extent we can be called spiritual. Spirituality in the proper sense means the expansion of our consciousness, freedom, and community, beyond the reaches of our present understanding.

The metaphysical view that allows for a realistic spirituality can be contrasted to one that renders spirituality impossible. The view of reductionist materialism is deterministic and does not allow for any kind of spirituality except as a comforting illusion. On the other hand, the kind of ready-made spiritual world that James attributes to idealism does not allow for the human spirit to be anything but a spectator or a passive beneficiary. James's view allows for the human spirit to do real work. Our decisions, attention, and effort make a real difference in ourselves as well as in reality. James believes that reality is malleable, and that a meaningful life consists in testing that malleability to its limits.

The Jamesian view of reality leaves room for divergent interpretations. But not every interpretation can be true. In "Pragmatism's Conception of Truth," James defines reality as that which truth must take into account. This means that a belief can be true only in relation to a reality to which the belief leads us. As explained in chapter 1, true ideas lead us to expect the perceptions that *really* occur and to prepare appropriate actions. We cannot play fast and loose with our ideas because there are things in reality that will help us and some that will harm us. We have to know the real difference and act accordingly. James's theory of *truth as a leading* means that ideas, which are parts of our experience, are true to the extent that they lead us to other parts of experience that we intend. And yet reality abounds with possibilities that overflow the actualities that we know. Our humanistic creativity consists of our ability to choose which of the innumerable configurations of reality to attend and thereby make *our* reality. Spirituality consists of our attending to those aspects of reality that we conceive of as being higher and better than others. The term "higher" expresses a spatial metaphor, but to call an experience higher means that it involves a more inclusive consciousness, greater power of freedom, and a more embracing unity.

Naturalism and Spirituality

Can spirituality be naturalistic? According to James, it cannot, if we understand nature as being the world that is seen and known by science. Science reveals a reality that is indifferent to human affairs and will inevitably destroy all that we had hoped for. A naturalistic spirituality of the romantic type remains illusory. We can live a happy naturalistic life only by abandoning any hope of the spiritual and living on the joys that life has to offer knowing we are free to end it at any time but living one more day "if only to see what tomorrow's newspaper will contain or what the next postman will bring" (WB, 56). So if the world as revealed by science constitutes the ultimate reality, we can find a degree of happiness only by lowering our expectation and finding comfort in the possibility of suicide.

But we may also admit that "our science is a drop, our ignorance is the sea" and live on the assumption that "maybe" the visible world makes up only a part of a much larger unseen world. Such a world might not only exist, but might depend in some small part on our beliefs and the acts which follow from these beliefs. The visible world can be interpreted as a sign of a larger world in need of redemption but having the real possibility for redemption. The existence of the spiritual world may depend on us and in James's startling phrase,

"God himself may draw vital strength and increase in being from our fidelity" (WB, 61). If our life with all of its suffering and tragedy does not signify a real struggle, a real fight, then life has no meaning. But, in James's words, "it *feels* like a real fight—as if there were something really wild in the universe which we, with all our idealities and faithfulness, are needed to redeem; and first of all to redeem our own hearts from atheisms and fear" (WB, 61). A meaningful life would not be comfortable, but it would be challenging, and James contends that that is what the world "feels" like; that is how we experience it.

A Jamesian spirituality does not involve an aesthetic escape from the world, nor does it mean wishful positive thinking in which we would ignore the evil and tragedy that abound. It means, rather, understanding the visible world as well as we possibly can, and taking responsibility for it. But a Jamesian view also means stretching our intention to the possibility of redemption, which implies a larger universe of which this troubled world stands as both a sign and a part. This view demands a deliberate act of connecting to the larger and better part to which we might give the name God. This act of attention, transfigures the universe from a dead unconscious force that remains deaf to our aspirations, into a living Thou who cares about us and our ideals and can help us to realize them.

While James rejects a naturalistic spirituality in the sense of a romanticized view of nature, his view of things that we call spiritual is continuous with the rest of our experience. Chapter 3 recounted James's example of getting out of bed on a cold morning, against all of our natural propensities. The will can overcome these propensities only if the intended alternative is attractive enough to overcome the propensities. This means paying attention to our goal with effort until it becomes attractive enough to get us going. Getting out of bed can serve as a metaphor for spiritual development. It means turning toward goals that do not appear to be as instinctively attractive as their opponents. Our naturally stronger propensities invite us to remain in our present condition; to prefer comfort and pleasure, to shy away from pain, to preserve the identity of our ego such as it happens to be. Spirituality by contrast means change, effort, giving up immediate pleasure, and most of all, breaking out of the boundaries of our current ego-state. Our present condition may be like a warm bed; spiritual development invites us with all of the comfort of a cold floor in a nineteenth-century New England winter.

The How and Why of Spirituality

Two questions pose themselves. How can we make the change? And why should we? To carry on the analogy of getting out of bed, the answer to the second question is that no matter how comfortable our bed might be we know that life presents more than this. "Some reveries of the activities of the day" will get a hold of us. So in carrying out the analogy, some spiritual need may motivate us to look beyond our life as it happens to be. But just as the severely depressed person does not get out of bed because there is nothing to get up for, our uneasiness with life may not yield any solution except a general sense of meaninglessness. Certainly there are people who are content with life as they find it, but such people probably are not reading this book. To write or read a philosophical work itself involves an effort that goes against our natural propensities, at least until habit makes it pleasant.

The other question, "*How* can we make the change?" means, how do we find spiritual values and make them attractive enough to overcome our propensities? The symbols of traditional religion can be the key. In "The Moral Philosopher and the Moral Life," James asserted that the belief in God releases all of the higher energies that enable us to live for our higher aims and aspirations. By the name God, James meant a being which is the deepest power of the universe and a mental personality distinct from ourselves. To believe in God means to believe that such a being exists and takes an interest in our destiny, a being who can hear our call and respond. Persons for whom this falls as a dead option have to look elsewhere or to give up looking and adjust to a world that provides no meaning beyond what they can find in the present situation. Persons for whom belief in God is a live option may choose to turn their attention to it and cultivate all of the accompanying ideas associated with this belief until it becomes the most attractive idea in their mind and the one that determines their actions and feelings. This constitutes the essence of spiritual development and, depending on the person's temperament, will lead to a life of quiet contemplation or a dynamic life of active benevolence.

In *The Varieties of Religious Experience*, James explains the role of the unconscious in this transformation. He had previously given some explanation of how transformation takes place on the conscious level. In the essay "Reflex Action and Theism," he shows that the human mind constructs a world from the infinite number of possibilities given in immediate sense experience. From the given contents of experience, we construct a world in the service of our volitional nature. As James says, "The conceiving or theorizing faculty—the mind's middle compartment—functions exclusively for the sake of ends that do not exist at all in the world of impressions we receive from our senses, but are set by our emotional and practical subjectivity altogether" (WB, 117). As described in the previous chapter, the theologian is performing the same kind of service as the scientist, artist, or business leader, creating a world of meaning from the chaos of possibilities provided by experience.

The theologian postulates a harmony between our volitional nature and the nature of things. This interpretation must be true to the impressions of the senses and to the second function of the mind, the reasoning function.

Because of the overwhelming number of possible sense impressions, there are countless ways to organize sense impressions and the selection and organization depends on the interest of the organism. The materialistic reductionist knows one way to organize the impressions and insists that this can be the only rational way. As an aside, the religious fundamentalist does the same thing. But James's radical empiricism insists that no object of experience can be ruled out a priori. So we can examine experience, as James does, for alternatives to materialism and religious fundamentalism.

In the "Energies of Men" James argues that the critical attitude blocks off the awareness of larger ideas whose effects would be what James calls "dynamogenic," a source of power. The contextual background of this statement is James's assertion that most people live and work far below their potential because of bad habits and ideas. Ideas provide the basis of action and certain ideas can stimulate extraordinary energy and action. But ideas can also serve to inhibit other ideas. He says:

> Relatively few medical men and scientific men, I fancy, can pray. Few can carry on any living commerce with "God." Yet many of us are aware of how much freer and abler our lives would be, were such important forms of energizing not sealed up by the critical atmosphere in which we have been reared.... One part of our mind dams up—even *damns* up—the other parts.[1]

This statement reiterates the point made throughout *The Will to Believe and Other Essays*, namely, that while scientists must be critical in the area of science, the critical attitude that some scientists take toward spirituality is not necessary for their science. James attributes the skepticism not to a clearer apprehension of reality, but to "the critical atmosphere in which we have been reared." The problem consists simply in the fact that some functions tie up other functions. Scientists often transfer the critical attitude, which is necessary for doing science, to areas where it is not appropriate. The facts of experience and the commitment to coherent reason do not require atheism or agnosticism although they certainly permit it. James compares the person who lets himself get tied up by his own ideas to an able-bodied person who ties himself up and does all his work with one hand. James asserts that the main goal of personal and national education should be to find ways to unlock the possible extent of our powers.

A Worldview Compatible with Spirit

James left his metaphysical vision unfinished, and given his pluralism, it never could be finished until everyone has had their say. But he did leave us with a vision, which, though unfinished, provides a clue to his fundamental view of the universe. To be consistent with his lifelong pragmatic project, his view must be one that we can put to work. This section will conclude with a sketch of how James saw reality and how it can provide for a natural spirituality.

Any spirituality implies a notion of consciousness that transcends the merely physical. For spirituality to be real, consciousness can not be a mere epiphenomenon. (The epiphenomenal view is that consciousness is a result of physiological events but has no control over these events and no autonomy.) Spirituality implies that consciousness has some degree of autonomy and independence from matter. But since James's radical empiricism does not admit of anything that is not an object of experience, and all that we experience connects intimately to matter, spiritual consciousness must also be continuous with matter. How can such a thing be possible?

James looked at the traditional notion of the soul as a distinct substance, created by God who is himself a substance distinct from creation. In this view, spirituality would mean the development of each soul in itself and in its relation with God. But James rejected this view for two reasons. First, he did not think that the idea of the soul explains anything. Second, this view leaves God, nature, and each soul disconnected. Relations remain external, as holds true of material things. James did not use this metaphor, but he might have said that the discontinuity would leave us in a world of spiritual billiard balls that bump into each other but do not become each other.

He explained his view in *The Pluralistic Universe* in the "Compounding of Consciousness."[2] Although we humans remain separated from each other by our organic condition, you and I can be part of a larger consciousness that includes each other and our neighbor. Units of compounded consciousness in turn become components of a larger consciousness. We might call the highest consciousness God. Intermediate ones constitute communities, which compound to form larger more inclusive communities. The notion of "compounding consciousness" is compatible with the idea of God as "Something MORE," explained in the "Conclusions" of the *Varieties of Religious Experience*. On its *hither* side the something more can be understood as our subconscious mind. On the farther side the "MORE" can be identified with the highest power in the universe, a real personal being whom Christians and other theists call "God." If this notion of reality holds true, full spiritual development can be summed up in three practical problems: "1, to 'realize the reality' of one's higher part; 2, to identify oneself with it exclusively; and 3, to identify it with all the rest of ideal being" (VRE, 384 fn). Solving these three problems involves a spiritual training that leads to a union of the divided self, a surrendering of the "lower self," and a complete conversion leading to a sense of joy, security, and in many cases a heightened energy and capacity for work in this earthly life.

If the view presented here holds true, what difference does it make? Although it might make some scientists uncomfortable, it poses no problem for science itself. In fact it might help explain the malleability of nature that makes science possible. But apart from science, James's view explains some human experiences that a reductionist view would not; for example, free will, community, and the possibility for real growth. Free will is possible because even though each person's consciousness remains limited by his or her physiology, consciousness transcends the ego and therefore the individual physiology. It also makes the belief in immortality rational. For although each brain will die, consciousness is larger than any brain. The possibility of community finds support in the affirmation of a level at which my neighbor and I already share a consciousness. Spiritual growth means overcoming the ignorance by which an individual remains unaware of that unity.

If a person could turn these ideas into real beliefs in the pragmatic sense of habits of action, that person's lifestyle would resemble the description of saintliness in *Varieties of Religious Experience*. The inner characteristics of the saintly person, of any religion, include a sense of a larger reality beyond selfish interest, a sense of friendliness with the higher power that enables saintly persons to willingly give control of their lives to the higher power, a sense of freedom and elation as the restrictive boundaries of the self break down, and a sense of loving and harmonious affections that enable the saints to say "yes" to the demands of the higher power. These characteristics are not merely intellectual convictions but heartfelt sensibilities. The practical consequences that flow from them include asceticism, strength of soul, purity, and charity. Asceticism is enhanced by the fact that the pleasures and pains become relatively insignificant. The soul gains strength in the melting of personal inhibitions and fears. Purity results from the disdain for anything that interferes in the harmonious relationship with the Ideal Power. Finally, charity comes from the melting of boundaries between ego and others. The saintly person is typically severe regarding his or her own lower self, but warm and tender toward others in spite of the other's weakness and sinfulness (VRE, 216–217). James sums up the qualities at the beginning of his lecture on Saintliness:

> The highest flights of charity, devotion, trust, patience, bravery to which the wings of human nature have spread themselves have been flown for religious ideals. (VRE, 207)

The study of James's philosophy does not make such beliefs and such flights probable, because it does not make them easy. But it makes them possible, and that is a good beginning.

Part II
Josiah Royce

Chapter 7

The Idealism of Josiah Royce

The juxtaposition of Josiah Royce with William James makes one of the most fascinating comparisons and contrasts in philosophy. On the personal level they enjoyed the best of friendship, and philosophically they opposed each other on some very key issues. While James insisted on the incompatibility of the idea of "The Absolute" with human freedom and with a religious notion of God, Royce argued that a meaningful notion of truth as well as human freedom and religion require a belief in the Absolute. James and Royce related not only as friends, but also as neighbors, and both were part of the first great philosophy faculty at Harvard, a faculty that set the tone for the development of philosophy in the United States.[1]

James brought Royce to Harvard and played a very instrumental role in fostering his career. Further, James's philosophical ideas contributed to Royce's thought in some important ways especially the pragmatic notion that ideas have a dynamic character and achieve their fulfillment in the action of the person who holds them.[2] This section on Royce presents his metaphysical idealism and the implications of his idea for understanding the human person, followed by his insights on ethics and religion.

Royce presented his fundamental metaphysical views in the Gifford Lectures, titled *The World and the Individual*, delivered in 1899 and 1900.[3] These lectures provide the necessary philosophical foundation for understanding his ideas on human freedom and on the relationship between the individual and the community. His approach to these questions centers on the relationship between *ideas* and *reality*. Therefore he asks as we must, what is an idea? What is reality? And, what is the relationship between an idea and reality?

Royce identifies four historical views about the relationship of ideas to reality, which he calls the "four historical conceptions of being." He identifies the first conception as "Realism," which holds that things really subsist independently of our ideas. The second conception, "Philosophical Mysticism," dismisses the multiplicity of things as unreal and believes that only the Self is real. The third, "Critical Rationalism," defines the real in terms of possible experience. The fourth conception, Idealism, which Royce himself espouses, sees the real as "that which finally presents a whole system of ideas." But to understand what he means by Idealism, we must start from the beginning and get a clear understanding of the alternatives against which he defines his position.

Ideas and Reality

Royce offers as the most fundamental metaphysical questions: "What is an idea?" and "How are ideas related to reality?" He makes a distinction between *ideas*, which the intellect holds, and *images* of things. Ambiguity abounds in the use of the word "idea" in modern philosophy. The empiricist tradition of Locke, Berkeley, and Hume, calls anything present to consciousness an idea, and distinguishes between simple and complex ideas. What the empiricists call a simple idea, namely, a perception, Royce calls an image. What Royce calls an idea of the intellect, the empiricists call a complex idea. To avoid confusion, we must stipulate what Royce meant by an idea.

An image of an object does not in itself constitute an idea of the object. In Royce's definition, an idea always involves *a proposed course of action* in relation to the object. On this point, Royce agrees with the pragmatists, Charles Sanders Peirce, William James, and John Dewey. The human mind does not serve merely as a passive receptacle of images; its work involves actively planning and executing plans. Ideas belong to the willing, striving, acting side of our life. For example, every scientific idea entails a program of action. The idea directs the scientist toward collecting more data, or forming the next hypothesis, or setting up the appropriate experiment. The practical nature of ideas also holds true of those ideas that we may have about such things as industry, politics, agriculture, and economics, as well as our personal ideas about morality, careers, finances, personal relationships, health care, and life goals. All of these involve courses of action.

Royce defines an idea as a state of consciousness that expresses a single conscious purpose. To be more precise, he says that an idea can be "viewed as at least the partial expression of a single conscious purpose" (WI, I, 22–23). For example, a simple state of consciousness, such as being hot or cold, becomes an idea if it leads to a purpose such as consciously deciding to put on or take off a sweater. Anytime we experience a conscious purpose, a desire or will to seek a goal, the conscious expression of that goal constitutes an idea. The idea serves as the first partial fulfillment of the purpose. The purpose first attains realization in the idea, then, perhaps, in the outer world.

An idea consists of a state of mind that has a conscious meaning. Royce explains "meaning" by making a distinction between the internal and external meaning of an idea. The internal meaning, the more fundamental meaning, is the *conscious* purpose of the idea, embodied in the idea itself. Conversely, any purpose, viewed as partially fulfilled through an idea, constitutes the internal meaning of that idea. We often have a purpose apart from its fulfillment. In that case we experience it as a longing, a yearning, and an unfulfilled desire. But when the purpose takes the form of an idea, that purpose achieves partial fulfillment in the idea. Partial fulfillment occurs when we get beyond merely longing and begin to make plans. The purpose to be achieved by the plan constitutes the internal meaning of an idea.

Ideas also have external meanings that consist of references to things other than the ideas themselves. Royce offers several examples. If a person standing on the shore counts ten boats in the water, the internal meaning of the idea consists of the fulfillment of the purpose to count. The actual boats in the water make up the external meaning of the idea. According to "common sense," the external validity of the idea depends completely on the object, which the idea must accurately report. The number of boats in the water seems to be independent of whether anyone counts accurately or whether they count at all. The objects that make up the external meaning subsist independently of the subject and the purpose for his or her idea. But Royce argues that only an apparent separation lies between the internal and the external meanings. Ideas become true or false only in relation to a consciously chosen task. For example, to accurately count ten boats presupposes that a person has selected certain objects, namely, boats within his or her sight at this dock. The choice selects what must be done, in this case, what objects are to be counted. Then, in relation to this self-selected task, the person might or might not count accurately and thereby have a true idea.

Solving the problem of the relationship of ideas to being requires a solution to the problem of the relationship between internal and external meanings. Royce considered the internal meaning of an idea to be fundamental and argued that we derive the external meaning from the internal meaning. He explains external meanings as aspects of internal meanings, and illustrates this with the example of a melody. "The melody sung, or internally but voluntarily heard, in the moment of memory, is, for the singer's or hearer's consciousness, a musical idea" (WI I, 34). The melody itself constitutes it own meaning to the singer. The singer fulfills her purpose in the act of singing, which constitutes the internal meaning of the melody. The external meaning might include many things such as the composer and the set of circumstances under which he composed the melody. The external meaning might also include the singer's memory of a beloved person who sang it. But Royce contends that the full development of the internal meaning would include all of the external meanings. The original internal meaning implies the composer who wrote the song and the loved one who sang it. The so-called external meanings fulfill a purpose larger than the simple singing of the melody. The apparent separation of the meanings that seem to be external to the purpose of the idea results from the limitation of our momentary consciousness. As a defect of our momentary conscious awareness, we often do not know exactly what we mean, and so our purposes remain vague. Increase in knowledge leads us from relative vagueness to determinateness in our meanings (WI, I, 39). Further development of Royce's understanding of meaning will take us to his definition of *being*.

What does it mean to be? According to Royce, "to be means to express or embody the complete internal meaning of an absolute system of ideas, a system which is genuinely implied in the true internal meaning or purpose of every finite idea, however fragmentary" (WI, I, 36). To use the example of the melody, the conscious purpose of singing might be amusement. But if the singer unfolds the complete meaning, it involves all that it means to his or her personal life as well as to the history of music. The biography and the history, in turn, have ramifications that branch out until they include everything related to the song and the singer. Of course, no finite mind can actually make these connections. Royce believed in an Absolute Mind who actually knows all the connections. The reality of the melody means that it constitutes an embodiment of this system of ideas.

Royce asserts that his theory of being has two main features. First, the nature of being and the relation between ideas and being depends explicitly on a theory of the way ideas possess their own meaning. This view contrasts with the view known as realism, which holds that we find the meaning of ideas in external objects that exist in absolute independence of ideas. Second, Royce defines meaning in terms of *will and purpose*. He does not mean that our will causes our ideas but that ideas embody our will. The process of *thinking* makes our purpose more determinant and brings external objects into internal meaning. The objects that seemed to be external are now seen as implied in the original purpose. The thinking process, moving from vagueness to determinateness continues until it reaches its limit. Being can be understood as the limit. "Being is the limit to which the internal meaning or purpose of an idea tends as it grows consciously determinate" (WI, I, 38). Being constitutes the limit to as well as the fulfillment of the thinking process. The artistic idea perhaps serves as the clearest illustration of the idea as both limit and fulfillment.

We find the meaning of the artistic idea in the expression of an artistic purpose. As artists proceed in their work, the internal meaning becomes more and more determined. When a work of art reaches completion, and the artist has achieved the purpose of the particular idea, then the idea has reached its fulfillment and its limit. Of course, for a finite being, there will be further purposes and further ideas to embody them. As Royce states: "Let my process of determining my own internal limit simply proceed to its own limit and then I shall face Being, not only by way of imitation or correspondence. I shall become one with it and so internally possess it" (WI, I, 38). So the artist and the poet are not merely copying Being, but are experiencing Being in the process of fulfilling their ideas. What pertains to artists and poets in a dramatic manner holds true in less obvious ways for any of us who fulfill the meaning of an idea by our action.

The First and Second Conceptions of Being: Realism and Mysticism

The meaning of "Being" and that of "Idea" cannot be understood apart from each other. Royce develops his thoughts on the relation between ideas and reality by contrasting his view to three other positions in the history of philosophy, realism, mysticism, and critical rationalism. Royce examines each of these starting with realism. Realism holds that objects exist wholly independently of any idea of them. Knowing consists of the process of bringing the idea into correspondence with the facts that are real regardless of whether or not anyone knows them. Royce rejects this view on the grounds that if things and ideas maintain complete independence from each other, there is no way they could ever be linked. If the objects stand independently of ideas the independence must be mutual, and the ideas remain independent of other beings.[4]

Naïve realism maintains that ideas copy reality. But ideas in Royce's sense, as the embodiment of purpose, cannot be copies. The artist's idea cannot be a copy of the work of art nor can the scientist's program of hypothesis and experimental verification be a copy of nature. Royce's interpretation shows the intimate interdependence between the idea and reality.

The view most opposite realism is that which Royce calls "philosophical mysticism." He takes as his model the teachings of the Hindu masters found in the *Upanishads*. The Western expressions of this view, found in thinkers such as Plotinus and Spinoza, are not essentially different. Royce examines this position experientially. He describes thinking as the process of looking for the whole of our meaning. As stated above, Royce contended that an idea expresses a conscious purpose and partially fulfills that purpose. But the fulfillment never achieves completion. Immediate experience of facts and the thinking process may stand in sharp distinction and even conflict. Sometimes,

the data remain obdurate, decline to be recognized, disappoint expectations, or refuse our voluntary control over them....Our situation as finite
thinkers is disquieting. We want some other situation in place of this one.
Our ideas, while partial embodiments of meaning, are never complete
embodiments. We are never quite at home with our world. (WI, I, 57, 59)

Mysticism seems to take us home. According to "mysticism" as a philosophical position, the goal of thinking is to find the self. The self in question is not
the finite thinker, the ego, disquieted in a world of incomplete meanings, but
rather the self that abides "free of the restlessness from which consciousness
suffers" (WI, I, 168). The self as sought by the mystic constitutes the restful
goal of meaning which now disappears in pure immediacy. The term "immediacy" connotes that there is no longer a need for "meaning" to connect the
self with reality. Unlike the ordinary consciousness of the finite thinker, the
self remains quietly at rest; it seeks no different situation, has no unfulfilled
meaning, and feels completely at home.

The description of the mystical self resembles nothing in our ordinary
experience more than a dreamless sleep. We may ask whether the Being that
the mystics seek means the oblivion of *nothingness*. Everything that characterizes consciousness is absent. No idea of "something beyond" stands as an
object of desire. The mystic desires nothing and therefore projects no "other"
as an object of desire. But the philosophical mystics do not reduce the
Absolute Self to mere nothingness as would be found in dreamless sleep or in
death, assuming no immortality. The Absolute is the very opposite of nothing.
Royce quotes the *Upanishads*: "To us, it is as if the Absolute in its immediacy
were identical with Nothingness" (WI, I, 170). The inability to distinguish
something below the level of finite consciousness from something above it
constitutes part of the delusion of finite experience. From the mystic's point of
view, ultimate reality is not given in ordinary consciousness; therefore we
might ignore or deny its reality. We, as finite thinkers, tend to imagine that
whatever does not make up part of our incomplete striving ranks as nothing.

The realists misinterpret the meaning of mysticism if they think that the
philosophical mystics simply attribute the realists' conception of *being* to a
single entity called "the self." For mysticism, the predicate "being" loses all
finite outlines and falls into pure immediacy. It cannot be spoken or even
thought. Since the realists think of reality as an attribute of many things, they
may incorrectly think that the goal of the mystic is *nothing*.

The inability of realism and mysticism to understand each other as anything but conflicting delusions reveals an essential characteristic of consciousness. The mystics have defined the law that "our consciousness of
Being depends upon a contrast whereby we set all of our finite experience
over against some Other that we seek but do not possess" (WI, I, 193). To

the mystics, the goal is the Absolute Self. When they possess the Absolute Self, they no longer need to seek it, and all ordinary finite consciousness collapses into immediacy. The mystics no longer experience any thinking or willing. The realists interpret this as *nothingness* because they note an absence of *real* objects. But the realist interpretation constitutes a misconception. For, although a person in the mystical state does not experience real objects, or think about, or desire them, the Absolute is not merely an absence. Rather, the Absolute Self of the mystic constitutes the goal of all finite thinking and willing. When mystics reach the goal, they no longer need to will or to think, but the cessation of willing and thinking has its meaning in the context of the goal. Royce explains this by using the analogy of the number zero. The zero placed between a series of positive and negative numbers has a meaning other than a mere absence. It is meaningful as a number in a series in contrast to and relation with other numbers in that series. So the goal of quieting thought and desire has its meaning as the fulfillment of the thought and desire rather than as a mere absence.

Royce demonstrates that contrary to what the realist may think, the Absolute of the mystic is the opposite of bare nothingness. It consists of the goal and fulfillment of striving rather than a condition that precedes striving or which connotes the absence of striving. Even if a restful dreamless sleep were the best example of the experience of the Absolute Self, sleep has meaning only for a tired person seeking sleep. As Royce puts it: "Annihilation is something to me only so long as I seek annihilation" (WI, I, 194). The philosophical mystic identifies Being with the goal of all striving. Being is attainment of the goal. The mystic denies that the process itself is Being. Royce, by contrast, maintains that reality itself consist of not only the goal, but also of the whole series of stages on the way to the goal.

The Third Conception of Being: Critical Rationalism

A third conception of reality provides a meaningful interpretation of both the realist's and the mystic's view of reality. According to Royce's third view, the *real* refers to that which validates ideas. This view defines reality as possible experience. Both realism and mysticism can be explained from this third view. To affirm something as real means that under certain conditions it can be known. For example, Royce cites the countless unknown meteorites in interstellar space. It would be absurd to deny their reality just as it would be absurd to imagine that the planet Neptune became real only when it was discovered by human astronomers. The reality that we attribute to meteorites means that under certain conditions, they can become known, for example, when they become incandescent as they are drawn into the Earth's atmosphere. In the same way, the reality of unknown planets means that given the right conditions of telescopic technology and astronomical calculations, they can become known. As shown by these examples, the real can be defined as that which validates a belief. The *third view* maintains the realist assertion that reality constitutes the objective standard by which ideas may be called true or false. Reality means precisely the ability to validate belief.

The third conception also includes the essential insight of mysticism. The mystic defines the Absolute as "the supposed possible goal of a process of finite purification of ideas and experience." As explained above, the Absolute differs from nothingness in that it validates the process of yearning and purification. The state that the mystic calls "Pure Being" expresses reality and meaning only in contrast to the process by which it is sought. The state of pure immediacy, awareness without the mediation of words, thoughts, or desires, validates the process by which the mystic attains the state of unity. To affirm the reality of the Absolute means that the Absolute fulfills the mystic's journey. Its truth resides in its validation.

To view truth as validity, Royce argues, is to surpass the realist's position that reality and ideas remain independent of each other while still showing reality as the standard for true ideas. We must ask whether this theory succeeds in showing any real relation between reality and ideas. Logic can show that reality has certain limitations. For example, the hypothetical judgment, "If A then B" means there is not A unless B. It does not reveal the real being of A or B. Likewise our categorical judgments "All A is B" means only that there is no A which is not B, but it does not show that A or B are real.

What about experience? Empirical facts can refute universal judgments by affirming particular judgments which contradict them. But experience of facts depends on our ideas. Royce points out that with the exception of the mystic, who seeks pure experience, all of our experience consists of "carefully and attentively selected experience." Our internal meanings are incomplete and take the form of asking questions. "They formulate ideal schemes and inquire, 'Have these schemes any correspondent facts, yonder, in that externally valid object?'" (WI, I, 285). The facts of experience can validate or invalidate our programs of thought. But the facts would not even be experienced as such without a program of thought. As in Royce's example cited above, the actual boats in the harbor determine the accuracy of counting, but the fact that there are ten boats depends on the project of selecting a particular area of water and counting.

Although experience can contradict universal judgments, it can never show that an idea has no application. It only shows that the idea fails in some particular case. "Hence, unless I have ideally chosen to stake my all on a single throw of the dice of 'external experience', I am not logically crushed by particular experience that this time disappoints me" (WI, I, 287). I can keep trying until my ideas determine that I ought to accept defeat.

To view reality as that which validates ideas does not yield a satisfactory relationship between ideas and reality; it merely helps us to put limits on the idea. Logic can make our ideas more determinate precisely by putting limits on them. We approach determination as a limit but never actually reach the determination. The complete determination of our ideas "is for us the object of hope, of desire and of will, of faith and of work, but never of present finding" (WI, I, 297). "Determination" in this context means the correspondence of idea and reality. So by discovering through experience and experiment the validity of one idea and the invalidity of another, we come closer to the unity of our ideas with reality. The lifelong project of thinking brings the whole structure of thought closer to the whole structure of reality.

Common sense poses the problem that if we have reality only as a goal we do not seem to have truth. For truth consists in a correspondence between ideas and reality. Royce therefore examines the meaning of correspondence. He first reminds us that ideas which correspond to reality need not resemble them. For example an entry in a ledger does not resemble a commercial transaction. Royce contends we find the meaning of correspondence in purpose. "An idea is true if it possesses the sort of correspondence to its object which the idea itself wants it to possess" (WI, I, 306). The truth of an idea cannot be judged by any external criterion unless its own internal purpose is known. Ideas serve as tools to achieve a purpose. Royce rejects the Aristotelian analogy that objects cause ideas as a seal causes an imprint on wax. We have ideas about the future which are true but whose objects do not yet exist and so cannot be efficient causes. Instead, Royce sees ideas as being as much volitional as intellectual. Ideas actively select their object.

Given the active and volitional nature of ideas, what is truth? How is error possible? The answer to these questions requires a further clarification of the relationship between the idea and its object. Royce states: "The idea seeks its own. It can be judged by nothing but what it intends" (WI, I, 325). Since every idea embodies a purpose, the object of any idea becomes an object precisely because the idea wills it to be. This seems to present a problem of subjectivism. If the object of any idea consists of what that idea intends, cannot a person choose whatever he or she wants, and will it be, by definition, true? To show that Royce does not hold such a subjective position requires a careful examination of the meaning of truth and error in his Fourth Conception of Being.

The Fourth Conception of Being: Royce's Idealism

In discussing the first three definitions of truth and reality, Royce concluded this aspect of his thought, as he often does, with a question. "What is Truth from an Idealist point of view and how is error possible?" The question of truth and error presents a problem because Royce explicitly states that an idea can be judged by nothing except what it intends (WI, I, 325). If this is the case it seems that there can be no error unless the idea intends error. Truth becomes whatever the idea intends, in which case the notion of truth is empty.

However, Royce believes that error is possible and that truth must be won. The answer to this seeming contradiction depends on the difference between the consciousness which we happen to have of an idea, and the consciousness which we would achieve if the idea were fully determined. As explained above, Royce defines an idea as the embodiment of a purpose. A purpose may be embodied partially or fully, clearly or confusedly, correctly or incorrectly. To say that an idea can be judged only by its intent does not mean that any idea is as good as any other. Royce points out that it is often hard to know what we want, especially when we are young. We can suffer from inner conflicts, self-defeating struggles, ambitions that don't fit our abilities, love relationships that don't work out. We may experience an "ill-defined vague restlessness or an imperfect conscious longing" (WI, I, 328). We must ask how the present imperfect state of mind relates to what Royce called the person's "own real intent?"

Royce builds his answer around the contention that a person's true intent constitutes a more determinate form of that person's present imperfect will. For example, a person may have a vague idea of success in love and work, but not know the person whom he would love or the kind of work he would do. Or perhaps he intends to marry one person and work in a particular career, and in fact finds fulfillment in marriage to another person and in a different career.

Every idea seeks its own explicit and complete determination as a conscious purpose embodied in one particular way. The complete content of the idea's purpose consists of the object of the idea. While we are seeking the object, and have not yet embodied it, we experience it as *other*. Once we fully embody the object, then we experience it as our own. We seek another as long as our own purpose remains unfulfilled. The search for fulfillment constitutes the meaning of truth. In defining a true idea Royce says: "It is true if in its own measure, and its own place, it corresponds, even in its vagueness, to its own final and completely individual expression" (WI, I, 339). I will illustrate Royce's thought with an example. Suppose a young man with athletic talent aspires to be a Major League baseball player. The life that he dreams of and hopes for is *other* than the life he is living, perhaps playing baseball in high school or college. The "final and completely individual expression" of the idea would be attained if he played in the Major Leagues. If, in the eyes of professional scouts, his talents do not measure up to the level needed for a professional career, and he never receives an offer of a professional contract, his idea will have turned out to be false because it did not fulfill its own goal. Suppose on the other hand, that before his clear idea of wanting to be a Major League player, he had a vague notion of a career in baseball. He now turns his energy to successfully becoming a coach or sports writer. Then his idea corresponds "even in its vagueness" to a true fulfillment. Therefore, although Royce holds that an idea can be judged only by its own intent, it is true or false depending on how well it corresponds to its own full and individual expression.

Since the phrase "full and individual expression" makes up such an essential part of Royce's definition of a true idea, the notion of individuality plays an essential role in understanding what he means by an idea. He calls an individual fact one for which no other can be substituted without some loss of determination. The final and true meaning of an idea consists of the embodiment of that idea in a way that is more determinate, meaning more specifically fulfilled, than any other possible embodiment could be. The fundamental question concerns the relation of an idea to reality, and for Royce the relation means "determinate embodiment." He defines reality: "What is, or what is real, is as such the complete embodiment, in individual form and in final fulfillment, of the internal meaning of finite ideas" (WI, I, 339). With the introduction of the concept of individuality, Royce's Fourth Definition of Being can be revealed.

The result of our exposition of Royce's thought up to this point shows the individual as the ultimate form of being. His conclusion emerged out of the analysis of the Third Conception of Being that identified reality with the object of a valid idea. This identification posed the problem that the idea of validity remains meaningless without an object to provide it with meaning. Any time that we are thinking, we look for an object other than what is now present. This statement obviously rings true when we look for some practical satisfaction. But it is also true when we work on purely theoretical problems. The discontent which drives us to work on theoretical problems stems from the fact that our ideas still lack the object which they seek. While we as finite thinkers strive to know an individual being in its full determinateness, the individual remains something other than the idea that seeks it. But for something to be an object for our thought, our thought must already intend it. Our thought defines the object and intends it to be our object. The object in its essence is already defined before we begin the process of thinking that leads us to know the object. The other which stands as the object of our quest constitutes the fulfillment of our purpose. Royce defines an idea as a state of mind that, at least partially, embodies a purpose. So the satisfaction of our will, which we now imperfectly embody in our idea, finds its full completion in the object that we seek but do not yet fully possess (WI, I, 346).

Royce contends that his conception of being brings together the three other conceptions in a synthesis. As in critical rationalism, whatever is real is valid, that is, it constitutes the object of valid reasoning. But the defect of this definition shows up in that it presents reality only as a universal abstraction and not as a concrete individual. The Fourth Conception agrees with realism that reality stands authoritative over our finite ideas. The First Conception, realism, attributes to reality the independence from our thinking which makes it possible for reality to be authoritative and requires our ideas to conform to reality, but it lacks the communication that would make it possible for an idea to know an object. Mysticism answers the problem of the isolation of realism by affirming the unity of reality with the true meaning of ideas. But Royce's conception takes into account the whole richness and variety of Being by attributing reality to the finite being in its longing as well as to the ultimate being in its fulfillment (WI, I, 358).

Royce deals with several objections to his theory. The theory states that reality consists of whatever fulfills one's meaning. Reality expresses "in the completest possible logical measure, the very will now fragmentarily embodied in your finite ideas" (WI, I, 358). If this theory holds true, we cannot expect our ideas to be impeded or contradicted by facts. What could be the nature or status of contradictory facts if we define reality as the fulfillment of our purposes? Common sense must make this objection.

Royce's theory, The Fourth Conception of Being, appears to be defeated every time our plans fail or we have to give up on something for which we had hoped. Some of the facts that affect our lives may fulfill our purpose, but many of them thwart it, and most of them seem to be indifferent to it. Royce phrases the argument against his own position:

> Who could for a day hope to hold your Fourth Conception of Being and still face a single one of the most characteristic facts of human experience, a single practical failure, a single case where dear hope does have to be resigned, an hour of darkness and private despair, a public calamity, or even a sleepless night, and not have this observation thrust upon him? Your reason is vain; these hard facts are against you. (WI, I, 374)

Royce, of course, responds to his own objection. He concedes that facts often defeat human purposes. But each fact can be looked at in two ways. In itself no fact is evil. It is only evil in relation to other facts. This statement expresses the traditional Idealist explanation of evil from St. Augustine to Hegel. But Royce offers a second explanation. While a fact that defeats a purpose is not evil in itself, it still defeats a purpose. Royce draws a positive interpretation out of this apparent misfortune. The defeat of a purpose makes us aware that the whole of being does not consist of this finite purpose.

"Loneliness and despair, just because they are dissatisfied, look beyond themselves for being" (WI, I, 379). Tragedy, death, or the loss of a loved person causes us to look for meaning and for solution to the problems and mysteries of life. We look for something that we do not have, something absent, something other. Royce interprets this longing as the desire for the Eternal. We find the meaning of death and finite despair in the search for the eternal. "Where then is that object? 'Not here! Not here!' cries despair. 'Aye, Elsewhere! answers our teaching, 'Elsewhere is precisely the true Being that you seek'" (WI, I, 379).

To recap Royce's argument, he holds that by definition, the real is the object of true ideas. As he had pointed out in the beginning of his metaphysical analysis, the relation between an idea and its object poses the fundamental problem. He identifies a relation between a partial meaning and a fully expressed rational meaning (WI, I, 431). Therefore, the tragedies and disappointments in life reveal the partiality of the finite ideas and point to the fuller meaning of these ideas. Royce based his ethics on the need to bring about the fullest possible expression of rational meaning. The following section will explain his idea of the human person whose task and whose very essence as a person depends on fulfilling his or her ethical role as a unique individual in the whole of reality.

Chapter 8

Josiah Royce's Concept of the Self

W hen we inquire about the meaning of the *self*, we ask not only about the self that can be *known*, but also more importantly about the *knower*. Who am I? Who is the knower? Who is the being trying to understand these ideas? Certainly, I can look at myself objectively just as I can look at another person objectively. I can see myself as an object of biology, or psychology, or biography. But the investigation of the self attempts to know the subject of all of these methods of objective inquiry. We can understand Royce's interpretation of the self by comparing it to some of the options that other philosophers have offered. The self is a substantial soul according to Plato, St. Thomas Aquinas, and René Descartes. David Hume, by contrast, saw it as nothing but a bundle of perceptions. Others considered the individual self to be an expression of a larger self, a cosmic consciousness, or universal mind. Such was the position of Hegel, and of the American Transcendentalist, Ralph Waldo Emerson. William James suspected that we are a part of a larger mind, which thinks through us, but did not think of it as an "Infinite Absolute Knower" as Royce held. While James feared that an Absolute Being would leave no room for the freedom and ethical meaning of finite beings, Royce unabashedly affirmed the Absolute Mind as well as the freedom and ethical significance of humans. Royce progresses from the popular understanding of "self" to an interpretation of the self as an ethical task. He argues that, contrary to James, the finite ethical self is compatible with the affirmation of an Absolute Self.

The Ambiguity of the Self

Royce begins his explanation of the self with an appeal to experience and ordinary language. An ambiguous view emerges. On the one hand we see the self as the source of our moral downfall. Words like "selfish" have a negative connotation as do words such as "self-centered", "self-seeking" and "self-absorption." We see self-denial as a virtue. So some moral teachers turn away from the self toward altruism. But this poses a question that calls the whole of ethical theory into question. If my self is worthless, why grant such importance to the other person's self? One proposed solution to this problem is *collectivism* in its many forms that have risen and fallen since Royce's time. An individual may be considered worthless, but a collection of individuals clubbed together are assigned absolute worth. In the twentieth century, most of the world has become disillusioned with collectivism because of the sad history of Fascism and Communism, and a backlash broke out in the direction of individualism. In the latter part of the twentieth century, many young people rejected altruism and collectivism and asserted that selfishness is a virtue and greed is good.[1] Royce developed his view during the late nineteenth century when an extremely individualistic capitalism competed with proposed forms of socialistic collectivism. Royce saw individualism and collectivism as two sides of a metaphysical shortfall which begins with an inadequate understanding of the self.

Instead of rejecting the self in a one-sided manner, we can see that even on the level of common sense the self serves as the source of moral worth. A counselor may help a client to see self-assertion as a virtue; a teacher might advise a student to "Be true to yourself." But affirming and being true to oneself does not mean the simple yielding to selfishness described in the previous paragraph. Rather it marks an awareness of the distinction between a higher and a lower self. The lower self consists of what we happen to be. To be selfish or self-centered in the negative sense means to be stuck with the status quo. It means to think and act as if this finite center of consciousness stands at the center of the universe and ranks as the ultimate good. Awareness of a higher self by contrast, issues a moral imperative to strive to become something else, something more. The higher self looms as the object of moral effort, and yet it seems to be something given, something discovered rather than something constructed by the lower self. The development of the self requires an increasing consciousness of what I am and what I can be.

In trying to become aware of the self, a problem arises because we have many selves, that is, many different social roles.[2] The self really consists of a cluster of selves. The notion of a higher self unites all of the selves at a deeper level. Selfhood can be seen first as a totality of facts. From the view point of another, my body, my clothes, and my actions constitute my self. From my own viewpoint, my self consists of the sum of activities in my inner life; a series of states of consciousness, feelings, thoughts, desires, memories, emotions, and moods. No clear boundaries separate self from nonself. If you tell me something or offer an opinion, especially an opinion with which I disagree, it becomes part of my consciousness, but I experience it as your thought and not as a part of myself.

The distinction between myself and the other person—ego and alter—constitutes the empirical basis for the self awareness. Regardless of the variety of experiences or their changing nature, each of us has a sense of unity and identity. Some of the experiences are "mine" and not the other's. The aware-ness of self depends on the fact that we experience some actions, words, and sensations as those of *this* organism that I experience as myself while other actions and words come from other organisms. The contents of consciousness that we identify as our own, as belonging to our own ego, include those that have the warm, feeling of coming from within our own body. These feelings are contrasted to the contents that we experience as coming from another organism through an external sense. As Royce emphasizes, "The most stable feature about the empirical Ego is that *sort of contrast in which it stands to the social world, literal and ideal, in which we live*" (WI, II, 266). Italics in original. However, the self as seen only in contrast to the nonself, consists of a fleeting series of experiences without any unity or coherence. We might perceive the self as having no other meaning and therefore become satisfied with David Hume's notion of the self as a bundle of perceptions.

The Self as an Ethical Category

But a philosopher might be convinced, in spite of the chaos of the tran-sient experiences of self, that there *ought* to be some principle with which to identify. The philosophers *ought* to find or create some principle for selecting from among the memory of past experiences and the anticipation of the future, some internal meaning which they grasp as their own. In saying that there "ought" to be some such principle, Royce does not indulge in wishful thinking, but rather he affirms a moral duty to find such a principle. Royce asserts: "The Self is an Ethical Category" (WI, II, 275). The self does not emerge as a ready-made entity from which we begin our life's work. Rather the self consists of a task that requires strenuous moral effort to achieve.

Royce rejects any realist notion of the self as a soul substance such as the type that Descartes held. Such a soul would be separated from nature, from its fellow human beings, and from God. In fact the soul would be isolated from the self in the case of a person who remains unaware that he or she has a soul. There would be no way to connect with an ethical imperative to which it ought to submit. The outcome would be the proud but isolated rebel or the solipsistic thinker like Descartes trying to prove that other beings exist. A person identifies a self beyond the momentary consciousness and identifies the self with a remembered past and an intended future. Royce contends that there can be only one justification for identifying with the larger Self. As Royce addresses his audience: "You regard this present moment's life and striving as a glimpse of a certain task now assigned to you, the task of your life as a friend, as worker, as loyal citizen, or in general as man, *i.e.*, as one of God's expressions in human form" (WI, II, 275).

We identify our Self not as a thing, but as an ethical task. Each individual human being faces the challenge of finding a plan for fulfilling his or her unique purpose. Royce's idealism strives to restore the individuality of the self in the face of modern philosophy which has made it a type. Royce's reference to modern philosophy includes any notion of a self or soul that treats it as a member of a class. Discourse about the self in general misses the uniqueness of each one. We accomplish the restoration of the individual self by seeing it as a life instead of as an abstraction. It achieves its individuality as a unique expression of a larger purpose that Royce affirms to be a divine purpose.

The assertion that the self is not something given but a task to be accomplished poses a problem. Must we not be something in order to even begin an ethical task? The answer to this problem lies in the distinction between a higher and lower self as explained above. A human is a thinking organism that can reflect on "itself." The self of such passive reflection consists of what we happen to be as a result of genetic and environmental antecedents. The higher self is not a substance but an ideal. To "be somebody" means to have a plan for your life which gives unity to your goals. Our own distinct life plan provides our uniqueness and therefore our individuality. We achieve this distinctness by recognizing our own life plan as different from others. Our individuality has a social basis. Without the social context of our life plan we would be mere types of the human species.

Royce recognizes a problem: an empirical study of the self shows a dependence on nature and society, that is, on heredity, temperament, and social relations. How can we attribute freedom and meaning to the self? Traditional philosophy addresses the problem of freedom by affirming a soul as the basis of consciousness. Royce rejects this solution by pointing out that if our soul remains a substratum that never comes to the light of consciousness as our own will and meaning, then it really explains nothing. He dismisses the soul as a solution by observing that the term "soul" would be a mere nominal solution that would in fact explain nothing. "You gain nothing but a name when an unobserved substratum is called a soul" (WI, II, 291). Like his friend and former teacher, William James, Royce had no patience with merely verbal solutions.

Royce developed an answer to the problem of attributing uniqueness to the self by affirming the world as the expression of one determinate and absolute purpose. The whole is unique, so each part is unique in relation to the whole. The previous statement looks like a fallacy of division. Does the uniqueness of the whole really mean that each part is unique? Royce's argument stands defensible. Apart from the whole, each fragment is merely a case of its type. An analogy might help to clarify Royce's point. Suppose a building represents a unique work of architecture. Then each feature, such as a door, window, or archway has a unique role in relation to that building. On the other hand, for houses mass-produced in a development, the windows, doors, and archways of each one represent types found in hundreds of others. In the unique building, although each brick, taken by itself, imitates the one next to it, in relation to the whole building, each brick has a unique role. As the brick depends on the whole building, so the individual depends on the whole society for its uniqueness. We all share a common life and derive everything from other lives except our uniqueness. Our uniqueness consists in taking an interest in our interdependence and in our place as part of the whole, and responding to it by our deeds.

The Individual and the Whole

What relation holds between the finite selves and the whole? Royce rejected the realist notion of the soul as an independent substance and also rejected the kind of mysticism that considers the finite soul to be swallowed up or extinguished in the Absolute. The question is whether Royce offered a third possibility and thereby escaped the dilemma of viewing individual egos disconnected from each other and from the whole, versus the notion of one whole that rejects individuality as an illusion. To escape the dilemma, Royce distinguishes between what the Absolute *is in itself*, and how it *appears to us*. From our point of view as finite observers, the Absolute appears as a goal, a fulfillment of a purpose. The purpose is to see our own lives as a meaningful part of the structure of reality. We experience a purpose apart from its fulfillment as longing, dissatisfaction, and incompleteness.

The Absolute life contains not only the realization of all purposes, but also an infinity of longings. Each being who experiences longing knows its own imperfection and finitude. Each seeks its relative fulfillment in another finite act or state. The Absolute Self includes the infinite variety of finite selves that are interwoven and in communication with each other. Each self consists of a unity that represents the unity of the whole, that is, of the Absolute Self. Therefore, the Absolute does not swallow up all of the finite selves, but rather includes the whole of all of the finite selves in their infinite variety.

There is no need to show that the finite selves somehow fell away from the Absolute as Plato and Plotinus had affirmed. From their own point of view the selves seem to have fallen away because they are longings. The longing belongs to the Absolute which can be seen either from the viewpoint of eternity where the ideal achieves fulfillment, or from the viewpoint of time when we finite beings continue to search for the ideal. Royce demonstrates the confluence of the two viewpoints by several analogies with ordinary experiences which span longing and satisfaction. A child's surprise at Christmas time includes the days of anticipation in which he expects the unexpected as well as the moment of the surprise which fulfills the waiting. Or we can think of the hiker who finds water after a long search and enjoys the drink while still experiencing the thirst. As Royce expressed the two aspects of the Absolute:

> I hold that all finite consciousness,—*just as it is in us*, ignorance, striving, defeat, error, temporality, narrowness,—*is all present from the Absolute point of view, but is also seen in unity with the solution of the problem, the attainment of the goals, the overcoming of defeats, the correction of errors, the final wholeness of the temporal process, the supplementing of all narrowness.* (WI, II, 302) Italics in original

In much of our lives we experience only the problems, errors, and defeats, as the child experiences the longing before Christmas and the hiker experiences the thirst. But from the viewpoint of eternity, both the striving and the fulfillment are real.

Royce answers the objection brought by philosophers such as William James who believe that an absolute and a preestablished harmony allows no room for morality. James maintains that morality requires independent individuals who may succeed or fail but each will do so on the basis of his or her individual will. In order to have a true moral agent, there must be the possibility for progress and also the possibility for failure. If real possibilities wait, then the moral agents can bring something new into being. There must be something that they ought to do and which would be left undone if they did not do it. James understood morality to be incompatible with the notion of metaphysical finality. Morality does not want to say of the world: "It is good," but rather "Let it be good." Morality gives priority to action rather than to contemplation.

Royce denies the charge that his system does not allow for moral agency and progress. Although wholeness prevails in eternity, purposes must be worked out in time. The finite consciousness knows the contrast between its own will and that of the world and strives to be one with its world. Its moral "ought" requires it to conform to a universal law. Those who rebel try to make the Absolute conform to them instead of they conforming to the Absolute.[3] The choice of conforming or rebelling does not depend merely on knowledge or ignorance of good and evil. Every act expresses both knowledge and purpose, and knowledge and purpose involve attention. Royce agrees with William James that attention stands as the central and constitutive feature of every act. According to Royce, as well as James, *attending to* an idea consists of an act of the will. If an idea sufficiently fills our mind, we translate it into an external deed.

We find the meaning of moral evil in turning attention exclusively to the private self as it happens to be now, and ignoring the other and the imperative of the moral *ought*. While Royce agrees that knowledge of the good compels our choice, evil consists of voluntary inattention. Evil consists of the narrowing of consciousness so that we do not know what we ought to know. Therefore the task of knowing and acting morally are fused not by denying freedom but by affirming it. The moral imperative requires us to pay full attention to the context of our unique role in the human community.

Royce argues that his system accounts for the life of the finite individual with its biological origin and psychological limitations, and yet connects it with the life of the universe. We can best understand Royce's definition of the self in the context of the four conceptions of being as presented in the previous chapter. First, Royce rejects the realist notion that the self consists of a thing among things; he denies that it is a substance. Second, unlike the view of philosophical mysticism, the finite human individual does not become lost or swallowed up in the absolute reality, nor does it strive to be so absorbed. Rather it finds its meaning and purpose in the unique role that it discovers in connection with the whole. Finally, unlike the way critical rationalism depicts it, the self is not a type. The self can be understood in the context of Royce's Fourth Conception of being as a unique individual that achieves meaning by its particular and irreplaceable ethical role in the universal order. Royce concludes that ethical terms constitute the only genuine definition of the Self. The unique individual wills himself or herself to be *this* person faced with *this* task, purpose and life plan, and no other. So while each of us requires unity with our fellow humans, with the natural world, and with God, we fulfill our role of striving for unity in diversity by contrasting our own self with the rest of reality (WI, II, 275–276). This vision of the meaning of our individual lives in contrast to, but in unity with, all else, enabled Royce to develop a philosophy of loyalty in which each of us serves a common cause by our own unique and irreplaceable service. Loyalty, when correctly understood, can serve us well as a foundation for ethics in the twenty-first century. The development of Royce's philosophy of loyalty is the task of the next chapter.

Chapter 9

Josiah Royce's Philosophy of Loyalty as a Basis for Ethics

Royce's Idea of Loyalty

In his 1907 book, *The Philosophy of Loyalty*,[1] Josiah Royce took on the task of establishing the basis for the whole of morality. He considered this the crucial need of his time since neither religion nor science has any worth without a genuine standard by which to measure their worth. Royce proposed loyalty as the ultimate standard. He stated his thesis in the opening chapter: "*In loyalty, when loyalty is properly defined, is the fulfillment of the whole moral law*" (PL, 9) (Italics in original). Royce undertook the task of giving the proper definition of loyalty showing that it can serve as the basis and the fulfillment of morality.

Royce begins his treatment of loyalty with a preliminary definition. In the course of the book, he interprets the meaning of the word in its ordinary usage and develops it into what he argued could satisfactorily serve as a foundation for morality. He offers as a preliminary definition of loyalty, "the willing and practical and thoroughgoing devotion to a cause" (PL, 9). The modifiers, "willing, practical, and thoroughgoing" are packed with meaning. Loyalty is a *willing* devotion. Your cause must be something that you choose rather than something imposed on you or something that you are born into without giving it personal consideration and choice. Devotion must be *practical*; your cause must be something that you act on rather than something that you merely feel strongly about. Finally, Royce insists that your devotion must be *thoroughgoing*; you must faithfully work through each step of a plan leading to the fulfillment or embodiment of your cause. Most essentially, loyalty must be devotion to a cause. Royce meant that your cause must be something outside of yourself, something larger than any individual, and must have value apart from any one follower. Consequently, the cause must be social in that you, as a loyal person, must have at least potential fellow servants of the cause.

The social nature of loyalty presented immediate problems for individualists in Royce's day, just as it does today. Royce anticipated this objection by exposing the connection between individualism and loyalty to show that they are not incompatible. As discussed in the previous chapter, Royce contended that individuality stands not as something given, but as a task that each person needs to accomplish. We are not individuals by nature. Each human being expresses an instance of a biological and sociological type and can be replaced by other people of the same type. We begin life as victims of our biological and social ancestry, "a meeting place of changing and conflicting impulses." A person can become an individual only by a conscious act of choosing a cause and a life plan to serve it. The life plan rescues the person from natural and social determinism to take a unique place in the community of humans. The *cause* provides the object of the choice and the plan. There can be no real individuality without loyalty. To be an individual in Royce's sense of the term means to be irreplaceable. Some readers might object that Royce offers a mere idiosyncratic stipulation. However, anyone who asserts individualism as a standard must be concerned with uniqueness. The affirmation that a person ought to act as an individual and be treated as an individual amounts to an affirmation of uniqueness and a denunciation of standardization. To rise beyond biological and social determinism and become individuals, people need to affirm something greater that governs their lives. It takes a cause beyond oneself to do this. An individual must express loyalty to some cause. For some, the cause that enables them to become individuals may be individualism itself. Royce pointed out the irony that much of the objection to the concept of loyalty finds inspiration in loyalty to individualism.

Because loyalty constitutes a necessary condition for both individuality and community, it is a prerequisite for any other good. For this reason, the greatest good that we can do for any person is to promote that person's loyalty. The greatest harm to people is to destroy their loyalty. Therefore, loyal people must be loyal not only to their specifically chosen cause, but also must be loyal to loyalty itself. *Loyalty to loyalty* stands out as the cardinal virtue. We each need to find a cause to which we can be loyal, but it cannot be a cause that destroys the legitimate object of someone else's loyalty. This qualification answers the critics who argue that Royce's philosophy would condone loyalty to an oppressive regime or a criminal gang.

Democracy cannot survive without a substantial portion of citizens who maintain loyalty to democratic values. Loyalty to loyalty supports all of the qualities which we rightly recognize as democratic virtues. Truthfulness, justice, benevolence, and courtesy express our loyalty to other persons and to the common ties that connect us. We could not survive as a democratic society without the virtues based on loyalty. As a specific example, Royce commented on business ethics in a free economy:

> In the commercial world, honesty in business is a service not merely and not mainly to the others who are parties to the single transaction in which at any one time this faithfulness is shown. The single act of business fidelity is an act of loyalty to that general confidence of man in man upon which the whole fabric of business rests. (PL, 67)

Therefore loyalty constitutes an essential condition of a free and democratic society. Contrary to a common objection, loyalty does not require an authoritarian regime nor does it lead to one.

The American Problem

Royce saw some specifically American problems for loyalty which sound very timely in the United States more than ninety years later. In Royce's time, as in ours, the national government did not always inspire much passion for loyalty. From our perspective in history we can note the emergence of some such passion during the two world wars and during the Cold War. After the Cold War, it did not seem likely that any leader could stir the hearts of the American people by appealing to loyalty to the federal government. For a decade there did not seem to be a creditable threat to the survival of the government. The sense of security changed after the attack of September 11, 2001, and the American people again expressed a strong sense of loyalty to our system of government. Danger from an enemy strengthens loyalty, whether the enemy is real or imaginary, foreign or domestic. The future of loyalty cannot be predicted, but if loyalty grows and diminishes in proportion to our sense of vulnerability, it cannot serve as a stable basis for morality. Although there may be no danger of running out of enemies, good policy does not create enemies in order to bolster loyalty. So we as a nation need methods of creating loyalty that do not depend on enemies. But at present, the degree of sophisticated cynicism does not provide an atmosphere in which Royce's philosophy of loyalty readily resonates on first hearing. His work met the same problem in his time that it would in ours.

In explaining the problem facing America at the beginning of the twentieth century, Royce cited Hegel's description of the Roman Empire and the absolute monarchies of the seventeenth and eighteenth centuries in Europe.

Hegel called this "the spirit estranged from itself" (PL, 111). He meant that the social reality seemed foreign to the people who made it up. The people did not see the society as their own; they did not feel at home with it. It loomed as a force from outside controlling their lives. Similarly, the government in the contemporary United States, except when it seems to be in danger, appears as an impersonal force and does not awaken a sense of loyalty. The lack of personal identification pertains not only to government, but also to the market economy. Economic forces appear as if they were forces of nature. As Royce described the economic forces of his day: "They excite our loyalty as little as do the trade winds or the blizzard" (PL, 113). We are more likely to be aware of the failings of our system than of its successes.

This attitude presents a formidable if not insurmountable problem for Royce's philosophy of loyalty as a viable basis for contemporary ethical theory in the United States. Royce contended that the great teachers of loyalty include imagination and grief. In times of defeat and loss, loyal persons preserve the beloved cause in their imagination. They grieve over the loss and the gap between the ideal that they long for and the reality bereft of the ideal. Royce offered Poland and Ireland as exemplars of national loyalty. Although today both nations are alive and independent, in Royce's time they exemplified lost causes.

The Contemporary Problem

Although the situation in the United States today does not exemplify a plight as clearly tragic as that of Poland and Ireland in the early part of the twentieth century, nevertheless we Americans may experience a loss. The divisions along the lines of culture, class, and ideology, and the general centrifugal disintegration inflicts pain on anyone who believes that America means, or at least ought to mean, something much better than what we presently experience. The gap between the ideal and the everyday reality produces a longing and can inspire the imagination to create what ought to be whether it ever was that way or not. Loyalty includes the ability to sustain the ideal and to work vigorously for its embodiment in contemporary life.

A danger looms that loyalty might emerge as a partisanship that fuels the flame of disintegration. This would happen if loyalty became loyalty to a part at the expense of the whole. The fear of partisanship makes Royce's idea of loyalty appear to be extremely difficult to accept. Loyalty appears to be a big part of the problem as it evokes images of everything from street gangs to private militia. But the solution to the problem, philosophically at least, can be found in the idea of loyalty to loyalty. For example, no one could serve the cause of the United States of America with an exclusive loyalty to race, ethnicity, class, or ideology. Such exclusiveness would be disloyal to the idea of the republic. An exclusive loyalty amounts to disloyalty to loyalty if it destroys the loyalty of its opponent. Loyalty to loyalty in the United States has to mean loyalty to the Republic. This means loyalty to the notion that diverse groups and individuals can live together in equality and mutual respect, and where we do not need a Hobbesian overwhelming force to secure the peace.

But loyalty to loyalty cannot be a bare longing for a nonexistent abstraction. It must be lived for and worked for in the lives of the loyal. Royce thought that we could compensate for the lack of loyalty to the national government by a reinterpretation of *provincialism*, a newer and wiser provincialism. The term "provincialism" poses a communication problem for us since the term has no meaning except a pejorative one in the United States today. I think that Royce's meaning can best be conveyed by interpreting provincialism to mean what we call "regionalism."

Writing while the American Civil War still involved a vivid and painful memory, Royce made it clear that he wanted to avoid the "old Sectionalism." By a newer and wiser Provincialism he meant:

> the sort of provincialism that makes people want to idealize, to adorn, to ennoble, to educate their province, to hold sacred its traditions, to honor its worthy dead, to support and multiply its public possessions. (PL, 115)

The regional loyalties mediate between the individual and the nation thereby overcoming alienation and increasing the strength of the nation through enrichment and diversification.

The Practicality of Roycean Loyalty

In the context of *loyalty to loyalty*, regionalism means that we devote ourselves to our own region, however we define it, with the hope that the other regions in the nation have equally devoted people. Granted, much of the American population is mobile and does not have a lifetime commitment to a place. The chosen object of loyalty could be the place where the person lives. If a person or family moves to another region they can become people of that region. National loyalty emerges as the larger object of regional loyalty. But loyalty to loyalty requires each community, whenever possible, to cherish and foster a similar regional loyalty in every other part of the nation. Loyalty to loyalty teaches that one person or community can do the greatest good for others by promoting their loyalty, and inflict the greatest harm by destroying their loyalty. This proposal also applies to national communities. While faithfully serving our own nation, loyalty requires that we act favorably to loyalty in other nations, as long as the loyalty is authentic and serves to build a loyalty to the whole human community.

What of the feasibility of this strong sense of unity? Royce's philosophy avoids being either optimistically starry-eyed or tragically defeatist. It demands rigorous action. In response to William James's facetious dismissal of idealism, Royce insisted that he did not look for a "moral holiday." Loyalty provides the motivation to work strenuously for the cause of unity. For example, Royce contended that the whole process of seeking truth implies that the world possesses a rational and spiritual unity. Any loyalty including the loyalty of two lovers to their love presupposes a unity that lies beyond the experience of any individual in isolation, but comes into view whenever two or more persons share a beloved cause to which they are loyal. He credits William James for helping him to discover that "all truth seeking is practical and that a purely theoretical truth that would not guide any practical activity is a barren absurdity" (PL, 151). Truth seeking serves an ethical purpose, to fulfill the eternal unity as much as possible in our temporal world.

Royce rejects the notion that the eternal exists by itself and that the temporal imitates it. In Royce's view, the temporal strivings and events constitute part of the eternal whole. Our actions take part in the process of winning the unity that we all want and need. Each of us as individuals has a unique role to play. If we do not do our deed, our deed will go undone and be missed. Therefore, Royce contended that his view calls for intense action rather than a moral holiday.

Defining loyalty in the light of his metaphysical interpretations, Royce concluded: "*Loyalty is the will to believe in something eternal and to express that belief in the practical life of a human being*" (PL, 166). (Italics in original). He contended that this definition applies not only to loyalty in the ordinary sense of loyalty to a cause (provided it includes loyalty to loyalty), but also to art and science. Science, like all truth-seeking, attempts to find the connection between the fragmentary bits of experience. Art also teaches loyalty. "Art supports loyalty whenever it associates our cause with beautiful objects...by showing us any form of the beautiful it portrays to us that very sort of learning and unity that loyalty ceaselessly endeavors to bring to life" (PL, 135). Royce's philosophical faith holds that in spite of the fragmentary and transitory nature of our experience, we can hope to find an invisible but real unity and goodness in the lifeworld. We can fulfill our ethical task to become a self only by developing and carrying out a life plan that enables us to contribute to the realization of the unity. Loyalty means the commitment to such an overarching ideal.

We must ask whether Royce has anything to say to those who do not share his metaphysical idealism. Historically, Royce had little impact on later philosophy, in large part because American thinkers saw his views as esoteric and dependent on a discredited idealism. Among other things, he sounded too German.[2] His view of truth stands in contrast to that of William James. The comparison between Royce and James's better known theory can help to clarify Royce's meaning. James believed that we can pursue the good and the true in part while facing the fact that something will inevitably be lost. We can strive to do good and seek truth now without achieving the salvation of the world. We can even seek the salvation of the world in the sense of preserving some ideals while recognizing that some ideals will be lost and that there may not be a final unity. We can pursue truth in the sense of believing true propositions to be those that lead to a satisfactory relationship with reality. Royce contended that James's theory of truth presupposed a unity, but Royce may not be convincing on this point. James did not seek truth as if it were a quality of the universe as Royce's invisible but real unity. James saw truth only as a quality of some beliefs; those that get us in touch with some aspect of reality no matter how fragmentary and fleeting. James's notion of truth did not imply a coherence in which each true proposition is connected to all of the rest. James hoped for a unity, an intellectual republic in which all things connect to each other. But he saw this as a task whose outcome was not guaranteed by an eternal mind and will.

Royce remained undeterred in making his argument. He neither ignored James's attack nor succumbed to it. Royce had argued in his 1885 book, *Religious Aspects of Philosophy*, that the possibility of error requires an eternal truth. His argument stands in contrast to James's position that a particular belief may be true in that it leads to the expected relationship with some aspect of reality without affirming any kind of eternal truth. Royce addressed James's position using another Jamesian notion, in a new definition of loyalty. "*Loyalty is the will to believe in something eternal and to express that belief in the practical life of human beings*" (PL, 166). This argument ought to have some weight with anyone who accepts the idea of the *right to believe*. The belief in the Eternal is momentous in that it can determine whether persons can unify their own lives through loyalty to the ultimate cause of unity. It is forced in that a person must either make this choice or not. Is it a live option? This question, of course, must be answered subjectively. It was probably not a live option for James since he was terrified of the idea of an Absolute and considered it unnecessary for ethics or religion. Likewise, to anyone with an atheistic and materialistic view of reality, the Absolute certainly does not present a live option. To anyone who believes in an ideal realm in any sense, religious or not, or for a genuine agnostic, the viability of the option should be at least possible.

What options does the contemporary reader of Royce have? Three main possibilities present themselves. First, reject Royce as most of the history of the twentieth century has done and go on to other things. Second, recognize that perhaps he was correct and therefore live and think in accord with his tenets. Third, suspect that he is probably wrong, too good to be true, but commit to a sense of loyalty as if he were right. This would be in accord with James's conclusion at the end of the *Will to Believe*, "Live for the best, hope for the best, and take what comes."

People who follow either of the latter two paths would live to create a unity in their own lives and to live a good life by any ethical standard. If skeptics argue that the second group is wrong because they betray truth by living an illusion, this argument begs the question. It assumes that Royce, and not the skeptics suffer delusion. But further, a Roycean may ask them, what constitutes an illusion. By what standard is it wrong to have an illusion? Loyalty to truth, certainly interprets living an illusion as a disloyal act. The statement that it is wrong to live an illusion implies that we ought to be loyal to truth.

The third group, those who are suspicious of the Eternal, but decide to pursue it, live by a tragic sense of life. They resemble the airplane crash survivors in John Wild's allegory, who land in the Himalayas and although they do not believe that they can reach a village on the other side of the ridge, and even doubt the reality of the village, nevertheless set out to find it. Royce compared our search for truth to the search for the *city on a hill*. He might be right and we may yet find it. In this uncertain hour we might concentrate on finding the mountain village. Some may seek it because they believe it exists and can be found with utmost effort. Others may doubt that any salvation exists, but recognize that the search for it may still be our best option. Persons who choose a cause that incites loyalty to itself and loyalty to loyalty live by a plan that enables them to become real individuals in real communities. Such a choice constitutes a significant improvement in the life of nearly anyone.[3]

Ethics and the Full-Breasted Richness of Life

The adoption of Charles Peirce's triadic epistemology, which goes beyond percepts and concepts to include interpretation, enriched Royce's thinking in all areas including ethics. All thinking involves a sign, an interpreter, and an interpretation. In Peirce's last letter to Josiah Royce in 1913, he expressed regret that his own pragmatism had provided only security from error, but did not provide "uberty," the full-breasted richness of life.[4] Peirce invented this term from the Latin word *ubertas* which connotes fertility and the abundance of nourishment that a mother provides for her breast-fed young. He described an ascending order of uberty going from deduction to induction, and then to retroduction or hypothetical inference. Deductive reasoning, which yields conclusions that we know with certainty, ranks lowest in uberty. Inductive reasoning reveals what is probably true in the world of experience. Retroduction produces a hypothesis that must be analyzed and tested. Security decreases as uberty increases. But Peirce had come to believe that logic should not only protect from error, but also should nourish truth, duty, and beauty. Royce applied the idea of nourishment to his own three principles; autonomy, duty, and goodness.

The triadic method of thinking allows an endless fecundity that corresponds to Peirce's uberty. Royce's thought goes beyond determining right and wrong in the sense of autonomous individuals fulfilling their duty. To merely do this corresponds to Peirce's security. But Royce, like Peirce, became aware that distinguishing right from wrong does not, in itself, fulfill the task of ethics. Ethical thought has the further task of procreating and nourishing goodness. Goodness implies more than autonomy and more than fulfillment of duty.

The notion of uberty connotes a kind of exuberance that, by 1913, must have been for Royce as well as for Peirce, a lost cause. William James was dead, Peirce lay dying, Royce had lost his son Christopher during the same week that he learned of James's death, and the war in Europe was imminent. But the notion of the good runs deep and consistently through Royce's life and work. In spite of James's insistence that Royce's Absolute provided a "moral holiday," Royce had in fact understood the good as that which we realize in the most difficult and sorrowful events of everyday life. Royce developed the idea of "good" in his middle and late works and applied his mature logic to help it to increase and multiply.

The task of the philosopher as Royce came to understand it, involves not only describing the good, but also aiding in the process of its creation. Good means the teleological harmony that constitutes the goal of every idea, of every life plan that makes an individual a self, and of every loyal act that builds community. The idea of the good expresses the full meaning of the divine-human process. Royce's notion of the good as teleological harmony is neither romantic nor escapist. Rather, teleological harmony develops in the world where good and evil struggle. To appreciate the struggle, to develop harmony, means to have life and to have it more abundantly, to be nursed and nourished by the full-breasted richness of life.

In 1898, Royce published a collection of essays titled *Studies of Good and Evil*.[5] The title of this collection shows that Royce considered good as something that cannot be known apart from evil. He did not offer a Manichean dualism but rather a belief that good consists in struggling with the divisiveness of evil and in overcoming it by bringing it into a harmony. Part of his purpose as he explains on the opening page of the introduction, is to show that his kind of philosophical idealism, contrary to stereotypes, is practical, empirical, and concrete. He writes:

> If idealism means anything, it means a theory of the universe which simply must not be divorced from empirical considerations or from the business of life. It is not, as many have falsely supposed, a theory of the world founded merely upon *a priori* speculation and developed in a closet. (SGE, iii)

In the opening essay, "The Problem of Job," Royce defines the good as the harmony achieved when evil is brought into submission. Evil consists of the chaotic disruption of the harmony. In Royce's words "...the only harmony that can exist in the realm of the spirit is the harmony that we possess when we thwart the present but more elemental impulse for the sake of the higher unity of experience" (SGE, 23). Royce had arrived at this conclusion by describing the human experience of good and evil in terms of those things that we seek or welcome versus those that we strive to avoid or destroy. Our understanding of good and evil depends on the kind of action that we are inclined to take. Yet our highest joys do not come from easily attained harmony devoid of struggle. In his analogy, the athlete could not have such a love of victory if it were guaranteed ahead of time with no possibility of defeat. The good life does not consist of abolishing evil or of ignoring it, rather evil must be subordinated and controlled in the harmony of the good.

Royce's understanding of good in relation to evil becomes more clear by comparing it to a similar insight of William James. In his well-known description of Chautauqua, James found the experience pleasant but empty. He preferred the city streets where good and evil mixed and victory was not assured. Both James and Royce realized that good does not consist of the pleasantness and security that would prevail in a real or imaginary pure world. But good consists in the richness that must include as much reality as possible. The world of Chatauqua included the sweat of ball players, but not the sweat of the laborers building skyscrapers and subway tunnels. Chautauqua was filled with decent people among decent people, but not with people trying to live decent lives in the midst of corruption, danger, and squalor. In James's phrase, the fullness of life involves holding evil by the throat. In Royce's more ponderous but no less powerful expression;

> One who knows life wisely knows indeed much of the content of life; but he knows the good of life in so far as, in the unity of his experience, he finds the evil of his experience not abolished, but subordinated, and is so far relatively thwarted by control which annuls its triumph even while experiencing its existence. (SGE, 23)

The full richness of life includes sorrow. Sorrow is not evil, and Royce identifies it as one of the teachers of loyalty. We may rightly consider the cause of sorrow to be evil. But sorrow itself teaches us to preserve the good at least in memory and hope.

Royce answers the problem of Job—the problem of evil—by showing that perfect being must include all reality including the imperfect fragments. Religious believers often ask why God permits evil; atheists assert that if God existed there would be no evil. However, Royce understands God not as a spectator who permits evil while He watches from the safety of heaven, but rather as an intimate being who suffers with us. Our suffering is God's suffering. In Royce's words:

> The true question then is why does God thus suffer? The sole possible, necessary, and sufficient answer is, because without suffering, without ill without woe, evil, tragedy, God's life could not be perfected....His world is the best possible world. Yet all of its finite regions know not only of joy, but also of defeat and sorrow, for this alone, in the completeness of his eternity, can God in his wholeness be triumphantly perfect. (SGE,14)

The perfection of good requires knowledge of evil, not just so that it may be richer in content, but more importantly that it may be more perfect in form and quality. The highest good subordinates evil to good in more inclusive harmony. When we experience sorrow we find it difficult to see the good as a whole of which our own life is part. But Royce maintains that philosophy has the task of helping us see the good, if only "through a glass darkly."

> In thought if not in the fulfillment of thought, in aim if not in the attainment of aim, in aspiration if not in the presence of the revealed fact, you can view God's triumph and peace as your triumph and peace. (SGE, 27)

Royce's philosophical idealism teaches the suffering person to see the continuity between each thought and its fulfillment, between aspiration and fact.

Therefore, ignorance, striving, and defeat, as experienced in every day life, does not lead to pessimism, which results in either succumbing to finite realities or denying them. Royce instead affirms the continuity created by achieving the goal and overcoming the defeat. To accept continuity involves faith. But faith must not be blind or irrational. Reasonable faith seeks understanding and produces the most rational worldview possible.

The rationality of Royce's view rests on the criterion that he employed to define rationality. He called the most rational view the one that accounts for the most experience in a way that is connected and steady. Royce's view accounts for the greatest good that one can imagine as well as for the deepest sorrows and the vilest evils. He does not merely juxtapose these opposites but integrates them in describing the process of a world in need of redemption, being redeemed, and manifesting the ideal of a redeemed world.

We must interpret the world at each stage of this process. Each interpretation yields new meanings that in turn become signs that require interpretation for further meanings. Our world of interpretation brings forth endless fecundity. Royce, of course, believed in Absolute Truth that gives meaning to the quest for true interpretation. But our limited view stands in contrast to the Absolute Truth as striving stands to a goal. Each time we make an interpretation, we intend to express the meaning that we would express if we knew the Absolute Truth. As our world of interpretation becomes larger, more inclusive, and more integrated, we progress toward that goal. Not that we will achieve it at some point in time, but that the striving and the progress are themselves an aspect of the Absolute Reality.

In *The Problem of Christianity*,[6] Royce described the "problem of the universe." The very meaning of reality depends on our need for interpretation. Royce defines the real world as the true interpretation of our problematic situation (PC, 337). If we did not see our situation as problematic, the issue of the real would not come up. But in fact "dissatisfying conflicts" mark our experienced situation. To illustrate how "dissatisfying conflicts" make us aware of reality, we can use Royce's own example of young people whose abilities may not fit their dreams and aspirations. They may be thwarted by the *reality* of their own limits and the limits of the job market. This conflict causes them to adjust their aspiration to "the real world." If we had no such conflict we would not deny reality but the issue of reality would not come up.

In our temporal life we experience the world as historical and teleological. "This endless order of time stands in contrast to an ideal goal which the world endlessly pursues with its sequence of events, but never reaches at any one moment of the time sequence" (PC, 382). Royce calls this endlessness the "tragic estrangement of the world" from its goal. Therefore the salvation of the temporal world endures as an endless contest with evil.

In the final exam in his last course in ethics, Royce presented a case that exemplifies the full rich meaning of ethics in the light of these insights. A young woman finds reason to believe that her widowed mother, to whom she feels very close, supports the two of them partly by embezzlement. This could be looked on as a moral dilemma in which the student has to justify the right action for the young woman to choose. However, Royce goes beyond the logic of mere security to provide "uberty," the full-breasted richness in thought. The reconciliation of the mother and the daughter presents the more important problem for the student of ethics. This case exemplifies the teleological good. A full act of loyalty does not allow the daughter to either ignore her mother's crime, if there is a crime, nor to condemn her and leave her all alone. She might find either of these solutions easier than working toward reconciliation, but each would leave an impoverishment.

The application of Royce's interpretive thinking to our contemporary ethical problems, such as stem cell research, abortion, and euthanasia would force all sides into unfamiliar areas. Each of us faces the challenge of remaining loyal to our own cause and yet trying to find a more inclusive loyalty that does not destroy the loyalty of our opponents. For example, a person devoted to the cause that we ordinarily call pro-life, believes in the sanctity of human life at every stage from conception to natural death. How can a person be loyal to that cause, and also respect the loyalty of the dying person who passionately believes in the right to be responsible for his or her own death? Asking these questions of course does not solve the ethical dilemmas. But these questions are likely to yield more fruitful answers than the more secure questions, such as which side is right and which is wrong. Without self-contradiction, we can think of a time in which there are no unwanted births and no abortions, no horrible drawn out deaths and no active euthanasia. But this condition remains so far from reality that even to mention these possibilities makes us sound like we have gone off on a moral holiday. We are a long way from such harmony not only practically, but even theoretically. And yet the role of the philosopher, if I interpret Royce well, requires him or her to be involved in the struggle to bring about such reconciliation.

In the example of euthanasia, such a struggle involves give and take, wins and losses. What do we define as the evil to be overcome? It is not death. Premature death is an evil, but premature death is not the issue in the case of euthanasia. Suffering can be seen as evil if the suffering remains meaningless. One side sees the evil as a loss of respect for life and the danger of a slippery slope. The other side sees evil as the lack of respect for the dignity and autonomy of the dying person who may want to choose his or her conditions of death. I suggest, as a Roycean approach, that although we cannot be satisfied with the current situation, the total defeat of either side would not serve the good. Each speaks a truth which ought to be heard.

The attempt at reconciliation would be discomforting to those who think of ethics only in terms of right and wrong. But Royce made it clear that the fullness of life is not a comfort zone. The loyal ethicists work toward the greatest teleological harmony. They do so by interpreting their own and their opponent's ideals in the light of the universal goal. Royce believed in the endless fecundity of interpretation and that we express our loyalty to this highest ideal not in dreams and romantic escape, but in our work and struggles here in the very actuality where our ideals appear only as distant aspirations.

Chapter 10

The Religious Insights
of Josiah Royce

I n the context of the present work, Royce's ideas on religion can best be
explained by comparing them to William James. Royce discerned connections, which William James missed, between ordinary consciousness
and the highest levels of religious experience. In his *Varieties of Religious
Experience*, James portrayed religion as a dynamogenic force but one that
could not be well understood in terms of ordinary experience. He examined
extraordinary experiences of individuals *"in their solitude, so far as they appre-
hend themselves to stand in relation to whatever they consider the divine"* (VRE,
42). Italics in original.

As biographer Linda Simon put it: "(James) set himself the task of locat-
ing those places where the 'ideal religion' forced itself into the real world's
details, to cause experiences—prayer, epiphany, or visions, for example—that
generated faith" (Simon, 309). A discontinuity stands between religion and
our ordinary consciousness of "the real world details." Religious experience
presents an alternative form of consciousness and has mysticism as its prototype. James defines the essential characteristics of mysticism as ineffability,
passivity, transience, and authority only for the one who has the experience.
The ineffability of mystical experience means that it cannot be expressed in
speech or writing. Our ancestors developed language to express the experiences of our ordinary waking life, and the mystical experience transcends
these describable experiences. Mystics may try to communicate the meaning
of their experience by poetry, paradox, and parable, but they testify that their
words are inadequate. James calls mysticism passive, not in the sense that it
makes the experiencer passive—it often has the opposite effect—but he

means passive in the sense that the experience *happens* to the mystic who cannot call it up at will.

The characteristics of mystical experience apply in various degrees to other religious experiences such as unification of the divided soul, conversion, and sainthood. These experiences are passive in that they happen to the person rather than the person consciously producing them. And like mysticism, these experiences cannot be explained in rational terms. Unlike the mystical experience, unification conversion and sainthood usually have a permanent rather than transient character, but they do not follow any known or controllable time sequence. Observers may know them indirectly by their effects, but the actual experience, although positively authoritative for the individual, remains opaque to anyone else. Royce by contrast, describes religious insights as communal rather than exclusively individual, communicable in ordinary language rather than ineffable, and explainable without recourse to the subconscious. In his 1912 book, *The Sources of Religious Insight*,[1] Royce defined *insight* as a specific kind of knowledge characterized by a breadth and richness of facts, unity and coherence of the facts, and personal intimacy with both the facts and with the whole. His general examples of insight include a successful businessman and his business, an artist and the details of a landscape, and a biographer in relation to the life of the subject.

Before applying the definition of insight to religion, Royce stipulates what he sees as the essential characteristic of religion. He identifies "the need for salvation" as the defining mark of religion. Religious insight therefore means insight into the way of salvation and knowledge of those objects that lead to salvation (SRI, 8–9). In defining salvation, Royce steers away from tying his interpretation to the teaching of any one religion, although he affirms that his idea describes Christianity and Buddhism specifically and could also apply to other world religions. Royce reached for an understanding of religion that grows out of the natural needs of all humanity. Among the various needs that human beings have, many people have a sense of some great good, a goal to be achieved without which our life is doomed to meaninglessness and failure. Further, we may sense that as naturally constituted, we stand in great danger of missing the good that we crave. Salvation means escaping the danger of the ultimate failure (SRI, 12). Religious insight consists of the rich, unified, and intimate knowledge of the great good that would lead to fulfillment. But religious insight must also include knowledge of the danger of loosing the great good and so the need for salvation, and finally, insight includes knowledge of the way to salvation.

Royce confronts his own development of religious insight with the "religious paradox." The human condition leaves us incapable of saving ourselves and so we need help from outside; this need marks the difference between religion and self-sufficient morality. But if our salvation depends on a revelation beyond our natural ability to know, how can we recognize and identify the true path? In the ordinary language of Christianity, without divine grace we are incapable of knowing God. But how can we possibly know the difference between a true revelation and an illusion? Royce observes that this paradox "meets us everywhere" and could as easily be called "the paradox of common sense," "the paradox of reason" or "the paradox of knowledge" (SRI, 21). How can we discern the truths of reason or common sense or knowledge unless we already know the truth?

The religious paradox haunts the progressive development of *The Sources*. Royce works out the dynamic relationship of seven sources: personal experience, social experience, reason, will, loyalty, sorrow, and unity of the spirit. The first two, personal and social experience increase our awareness of the good that we long for, but also increase our consciousness of missing the good. We seek the answer in reason and will. These, like the first two insights are indispensable for leading us past themselves; but we find true insight only in the last three, loyalty, sorrow, and the unity of the spirit.

Individual Experience

Royce begins with the inner experience of the individual and affirms that his position on the subject agrees with James's postulate of the experience of the individual "alone with the divine." But while James bases his whole study on this foundation, Royce describes it as, "the most elementary and intimate, but also the crudest and most capricious source of religious insight" (SRI, 27). Royce presents it as the first of the *sources* to show both its value and its limitations.

Each of us in our solitude may experiences the Ideal, the Need for salvation, and the awareness of a Deliverer. The *Ideal* represents the standard by which we measure the value of our own personal lives; we experience the *Need* as the awareness in which we fall short of the ideal or are cut off from it. The *Deliverer* must be something or someone who satisfies our need and enables us to achieve or come into contact or unity with the Ideal. Insight begins with the intense, intimate, experience of individual ideals. Individual ideals, however, remain diverse, changing, and capricious. Chaos abounds not only among various individuals, but even within the life of each individual. Through chaos, which we experience in ourselves and in the observation of others, we become aware of our Need. We become aware of the Ideal, which reveals itself negatively through its absence.[2]

The variety, transience, and capriciousness of our individual feelings reveal the Ideal and the Need in a single insight. The Ideal involves overcoming chaos and achieving a unity of ideals as well as the self-possession that would accompany such a spiritual unity. The power and presence that would give unity to the chaotic elements must be something that transcends the limits of our personal experience. The narrowness, transience, and fragmentation of our individual life reveal the need for salvation. We see our various interests one at a time, and we live many lives lacking in harmony with each other. Each interest has its own plan but the interests press on inconsistently with each other. Over a lifetime we experience disparity, whether we interpret it as our youth having an unrealistic foundation for our mature reality, or our mature activities betraying our youthful ideals. Many tragedies of life result from our narrowness of vision. To illustrate Royce's observation, we can imagine a thirty year old job applicant, struggling to find a career path, who regrets that he put all of his youthful energy into an unsuccessful attempt at an athletic career; or a sales manager who wonders if she gave up too soon on her dream of being a concert cellist. Whether we look at our life day by day or over the long run, we realize that we "thwart our own plan by our fickleness" (SRI, 49).

Salvation from this condition consists of a wider vision that enables us to "see life steadily and see it whole, and then to live triumphantly in the light of that vision" (SRI, 50). The larger vision that disrupts our narrowness may come from a tragic event in our life. For example, the death of a loved one, a lost love, or a career failure, may remind us of the opportunities that we lost while pursuing some fragmentary bits of our life. As Royce describes the origin of these insights:

> Such moments of insight come to us sometimes when our friends die, and when memory reminds us of our neglected debts of love or of gratitude to them...they are, I repeat, often tragic moments. But they enlighten, and they show us our need. (SRI, 50)

Royce identifies this kind of expanded vision as a religious insight that popular language often refers to as "understanding the will of God." Such insight does not depend on an intrusion from above nor from an upsurge from the subconscious. It appears as a conscious and rational view of what our life would be if it overcame its narrowness and fickleness. The social world expands wider than that of any individual, and the ability to understand and share another's point of view corrects our own narrowness. Further, our social responsibility imposes a discipline that moderates our capriciousness.

Social Experience

Two very diverse experiences, guilt and friendship, clearly demonstrate how social existence guides us toward salvation. We experience guilt as isolation and loneliness, a negative way to salvation. The experience of guilt makes us feel as outcasts from all human sympathy. Royce cites the examples of Coleridge's Ancient Mariner and Dostoyevsky's Raskolnikov in *Crime and Punishment*. Fundamental guilt grows out of an awareness of a greatest good, and the recognition of missing it. The absence of a desired good and a sense of irrevocable loss provoke the awareness of the need for salvation. The sense of failure as a human being separates the guilty person from human society. If redemption is possible, we experience it as reconciliation with the human community.

Friendship stands as a more obvious and direct way to become aware of salvation. The friend or the beloved person reveals a vision of what life should be. Friendship or love between two persons constitutes a microcosm of human existence when it has overcome its narrowness and capriciousness. We can overcome narrowness by seeing the other as being at least as valuable as our self. Fidelity and loyalty to friends serve as the antidote to the capriciousness of the individual alone. But particular communities, which exist at times among groups of friends, fall short of social existence in the larger sense. Narrowness and capriciousness assert themselves within groups, between groups, and in society at large. The experience of unity, stability, and wholeness found in friendship, like that found in the yearning of the guilty person, provides only a glimpse of salvation. Society itself needs salvation. Personal and social experience intensifies our awareness of the great good. But the danger of missing the good and the need for salvation also intensify. The search, therefore, must go further and Royce turns to "the office of reason."

Reason

Many empiricists, including James, place reason in opposition to experience and hold that reason cannot be the source of insight. Such empiricists limit reason to sorting out the data of experience. Its duties and competencies include only technical jobs such as recording, analyzing, computing, and teaching. Royce dismisses this position by arguing that reason has an office larger than mere abstraction and analysis. Properly understood, reason does not stand opposed to empirical experience or intuition, and, in fact, constitutes a source of insight. Royce appeals to ordinary language to develop the full meaning of reason. When we describe a person as unreasonable, we usually do not mean that the person suffers a deficiency in the power of abstraction and analysis. Rather, we mean that the person sees only a narrow slice of existence, usually his or her own momentary self-interest. To be reasonable means to see the big picture, which includes many things at once and their relation to each other. Royce offers as a definition of reason: "the power to see widely, steadily, and connectedly" (SRI, 87). The opposite of reason is not intuition but narrowness of vision that limits the mind to only one aspect of a situation or to capriciously wander from one aspect to another without seeing the connection or context.

Intuition and reason are not opposed, but an opposition stands between inarticulate intuition and articulate insight. Royce's definition of "insight" includes a wide range of empirical data, intimate personal intuition, and the unifying role of reason. Therefore the term "articulate insight" involves experience, intuition, and reason. Experience may be narrow or broad, fragmentary or unified. Royce calls narrow or fragmentary experience "blind." He places blind experience in opposition to broad, unified experience, which he calls "rational." The role of reason broadens the scope of experience through abstraction and generalization. Further, reason connects the parts into wholes which can be understood and articulated. Reason does not stand opposite or adjacent to intuition and experience. Rather, reason exhibits the power to create wholes from the fragments of intuition and experience and thereby introduce the novelty of articulate insight.

The empiricists had emphasized the analytic role of reason and denied that reason could provide any new knowledge. Royce proposes that reason has a synthesizing function, which by discovering relationships and forming synoptic unities, provides new insights. Forming abstractions does not constitute the final purpose of reason. Abstractions serve to facilitate the unified view of large and various entities that human consciousness could not otherwise handle. For example, a married couple know each other and know their children in a very concrete way while words such as "couple," "children," and "family" represent abstractions. But the abstractions enable the couple to understand themselves and their relation to the whole human community in a way that they could not do without the abstractions. They do not have to choose between intimate knowledge and intellectual knowledge but can enjoy both.

In religious matters too, we never have to choose between the barren abstractions of reason and the inarticulate upsurges from the unconscious. The need to make such a choice represents the Jamesian position that Royce opposes. For an experience to be a religious insight, it must involve not only wide experience and deep intuitive intimacy, but also requires unification and articulation. Religious insight, like any insight, must be, by definition, rational.

Royce's analysis of the office of reason cannot avoid the religious paradox. He reminds the reader of the paradox and how its pervasiveness shows up in this context as the "paradox of reason." When our reasoned opinions contradict the opinions of another, we know that at least one of us must be in error and so human reason is fallible. We strive to adjudicate conflicts by use of reason, but the fallibility of reason becomes the source of the problem. Royce appeals to one of his earliest philosophical insights, namely, that the very possibility of error implies a universal truth. When we express an opinion, we imply that our view would be affirmed by a larger insight, one that knew all the facts relevant to the question that we try to answer. Every true opinion would be part of the universal insight; every error would be contradicted by the universal insight. A universal insight implies a universal knower who in ordinary language we call God. Since no human individual knows even "the common sense of mankind" much less the universal insight, our appeal must be to a knower beyond our experience and our knowledge. Royce, therefore, calls reason a genuine religious insight, but one that remains too abstract and contemplative to satisfy our religious need for salvation (SRI, 115–1116).

Will

While emphasizing that religious insight must be rational, Royce insists equally that insight does not belong to the passive intellectual spectator. Royce challenges his own position by observing that even if we could view the whole world as an object of divine insight, we must ask "how does such a view give a man the power to live more reasonably than he otherwise would?" (SRI, 129). He notes James's charge that any passive idealistic notion is futile, "thin," and has as its only pragmatic function to justify a moral holiday. Royce concurs with James's pragmatic view that an opinion can be meaningful only if it guides the will to some particular course of action. Will, as well as reason, ranks as a source of religious insight. "No truth is a saving truth—yes, no truth is a truth at all unless it guides and directs life" (SRI, 144). Royce confirms the notion that ideas involve an attitude of the will that means preparation for action. And he agrees that the verification of the idea resides in the consequences of the idea worked out in the plan of action.

After his presentation of the individual, social, rational, and volitional sources of insight, Royce acknowledges that readers may rightly claim that the treatment so far remains mere philosophy and does not provide them with the insight to meet the needs that the philosophical analysis uncovered. In short, it does not yet meet the religious need for salvation. How do we find a way to personal salvation through union with other people? We need not only to fulfill the rational need for a unified view of the world, but we need to find a way to make our wills conform to it so as to act on the insight. The Religious Paradox forces an even tougher question; how can we discern the "will of God" from our personal or social caprices? Royce addresses these problems in the "religion of Loyalty."

Loyalty

Royce sees religious awareness as a sense of personal imperfection, a danger of losing the greatest good, and a need for a deliverer. Nonreligious moralists believe that they can do what they must by their own effort. By contrast, a nonmoral religion would be either superstition or a kind of barren aestheticism which Royce despised as much as James did. Royce, however, describes a religious morality that integrates *religion and morality*.

> There is a sort of consciousness which equally demands of those whom it inspires, spiritual attainment and strenuousness, serenity and activity, resignation and vigour, life in the spirit and ceaseless enterprise in service. (SRI, 181)

Royce considers this kind of consciousness as neither oxymoronic nor reserved to a few highly cultivated souls. We can find such consciousness among the most obscure and unlearned people. Royce cites a newspaper story of a lighthouse keeper, Ida Lewis. When her husband died, she not only faithfully kept the light burning, but in case of shipwreck, she often risked her own life to rescue those in danger, and in her long career saved eighteen sailors from drowning. Other examples that Royce cites are mothers, warriors, patriots, martyrs, lovers, and scientists. They have in common a loyalty to their cause. Social interests can be capricious as can individual motives. Reason and will taken together can overcome the narrowness and capriciousness but to attain this integration, people need a Cause to which they can be loyal.

Loyal people are not altruistic and forgetful of self. Rather, they assert themselves as strong, well-developed individuals. As Royce said in the example of the lighthouse keeper, if you find yourself in danger of drowning, you hope for a rescuer who has enjoyed developing her boating skills and takes just pride in her achievement. The more of a self she has, the more she has to help you with. Such a person also has strong social motives. For the rescuer, the mother, the warrior, and the scientist, developing and expressing themselves goes hand in hand with serving others. They could not do one without the other.

Royce introduces the religious element into loyalty by identifying the Cause as a free gift, a grace. It needn't be overtly religious, and the servant of the cause may be emphatically atheistic. But the Cause must involve something such as the quest for scientific truth, which we recognize as bigger than any person, which unites the lives of many in a common quest, and which we experience as something not of and for the ego, but something that we dis-cover and serve. Of course devotion to a cause can be narrow and capricious as in loyalty to a criminal gang or a hate group. But as Royce had argued in *The Philosophy of Loyalty*, the loyal person must respect the loyalty of others and the truly loyal person stands loyal to loyalty itself. The moral imperative is "Be Loyal;" and "So be loyal to your own cause as thereby to serve the advancement of the cause of universal loyalty" (PL, 202). The goal of a truly loyal person is the spiritual unity of every rational being. This goal constitutes the Cause of Causes.

A Cause can never be revealed to us unless we already have a love for the unity of spiritual life. "This presence will come to you in a beloved form, as something human, dear, vitally fascinating." It may be the face of a beloved person or a beloved community. The Cause requires volition and effort once you have chosen it. But you cannot choose it until you discover it, and so the Cause expresses will *and* grace, morality *and* religion. The religion of loyalty constitutes an insight that integrates the insights of personal need for salvation, the social sense, reason and will.

In describing the heroic loyalty of Ida Lewis, Royce cited another story of a woman lighthouse keeper. Her husband, who was the lighthouse keeper died when he took his boat out in a storm to attempt to save shipwrecked sailors. The storm continued for three days and the widow, in spite of her own grief, climbed the stairs of the tower each evening to make sure the light continued to shine for other sailors. She continued to do this on her own until the government appointed her as the official keeper. She spent the rest of her life keeping the lighthouse. Royce refers several times to the lighthouse as an emblem for loyalty. The loyal person keeps the light burning in the face of storm, personal loss, and grief. The link between loyalty and sorrow evokes the next great *source of religious insight*.

Sorrow

The reality of evil poses one of the greatest paradoxes facing any reli-gious philosophy. If evil is vincible or even illusory, then we have no need for salvation, and no need for religion as Royce defines it. On the other hand if evil is triumphant, then religion remains illusory and salvation impossible. Royce identifies as the essential characteristic of religion and specifically of Christianity, the experience of real tragedy *and* the hope of salvation. So while Royce, here, passes over pleasant things like beauty and love of nature as *sources,* he presents as his sixth *source* of insight, sorrow.

Royce does not equate sorrow with evil but he begins his consideration of sorrow with a general account of evil and the natural human reaction to it.

Humans have a very strong urge to destroy evil and that urge motivates much of our behavior. Every nation's folklore gives first place to the warrior and admires him precisely because he eradicates evil by killing the enemy. Even in areas other than war we think in terms of destruction of ills; we honor the *fight* against disease or the *eradication of* ignorance, racism, and poverty. The hero as a destroyer becomes the model for our highest moral thinking. Every moral opinion depends on a judgment about what should be destroyed; differences of opinions on moral issues consist of differences concerning what ought to be destroyed.

Religion differs from morality in that the religious quest for salvation includes a "communion with the master of life" and an effective appeal to principles that connect us to the "whole nature of things" (SRI, 220). So although religion sees the ills as a real danger to salvation, the saving force ultimately prevails as stronger. In Royce's development of the *Sources*, he had argued that the caprices of our personal and social lives find their meaning in a unity of reason and will only when loyalty to a cause reveals that the ultimate nature of reality consists of a spiritual unity. But if the cause of spiritual unity is a mere illusion, then all of our human causes remain subjects of chance just as do our own caprices. We may still feel the need for salvation and may struggle with whatever we consider evil, but the world that we thought religious insight had revealed, would, in fact, not be real (SRI, 22). Our awareness of the massiveness of evil can easily lead us to conclude the unreality of religious insight. Royce presents the dilemma that challenges religion.

> Either the evil of the world is of no great importance, and then religion is useless; or the need of salvation is great and the way is straight and narrow; and then evil is deeply rooted in the very nature of reality and religion seems a failure. (SRI, 227)

Royce, typically, presents a strong argument against his own position and describes the problem of evil for more than twenty pages without showing how it can be the basis of religious insight.

The insight dawns with the awareness that the common moral imperative, "Evil ought to be put out of existence," does not reveal the whole reality of evil and our relationship to it. Sometimes ills are so inseparably bound with the good that we cannot simply destroy them without destroying the good that we love. We overcome such ills only by assimilating and idealizing them, thereby transforming them from mere ills in need of destruction to cherished parts our own life plan and our vision of the whole. Our attitude of assimilating and idealizing ills constitutes "the highest level of reasonableness." We supercede our role as "man the destroyer" and become "man the creator" as we learn to "substitute growth for destruction and creative assimilation for barren hostility" (SRI, 236). The religious insight reveals our own power to assimilate and idealize ills, and gives us a hint as to how the larger spiritual process works in the world.

An example of the distinction between an ill that should be destroyed and one that must be assimilated and idealized occurs when we are in danger of losing a loved one. We do everything in our power to prevent the loss by eradicating the disease or life-threatening situation. But if we have lost a loved one, we do not wish to be anesthetized against the pain and suffering. This is true not only of a lost life, but also of a lost love or a lost cause. The sorrow that we feel expresses the love that was so important to us. "Sorrow" is the name that Royce gives to idealized and assimilated ills. In defining sorrows, Royce refers to them as:

> ...the ills that one rationally faces only when one, through some essentially active, constructive, moral process, creatively assimilates and idealizes them, and thus wins them over to be part of the good—not when one merely drives them out of existence. (SRI, 239)

Royce had said that loyalty was "by far the most important" of the *sources,* and the loyal spirit reveals itself only by being steadfast in the face of difficulties and tragedy. There could be no loyalty in a world in which the loyal person met no adversity. In *The Philosophy of Loyalty,* he named grief as one of the teachers of loyalty. Grief shows us that we do not find happiness in our present condition, and therefore we have a need for salvation. The spirit of loyalty sustains the hope of salvation.

Unity of the Spirit

In the final section of *The Sources,* "The Unity of the Spirit and the Invisible Church," Royce articulates what he considers to be the heart and core of every higher religion. Our human sorrows include the limitation of our consciousness. We can be aware of only a few fragmentary things at any one time, and we yearn for a vision of the whole. An intimate knowledge of many things integrated as a unity constitutes the definition of "insight" that Royce presented at the beginning of *Sources.* To achieve the unity that constitutes knowledge and insight we have to go beyond direct perception and depend on indirect knowledge gained through memory, habit, and abstraction. Royce illustrates this with the perception of the smell of a flower or the glimpse of a face, each of which we connect with many associations and generalizations that make it part of a unified world of knowledge. But our knowledge remains ever incomplete and we form opinions that we believe to be true. Royce insists that an assertion is true only if there is a larger consciousness to which the opinion of our partial consciousness conforms. The unity of meanings that belong to the implied larger consciousness Royce calls "the unity of the spirit." The awareness of the unity of the spirit gives us a glimpse of a reality that transcends the consciousness of any human being and thereby enables us to share in the larger unity. But in Royce's account of our sharing in the "supernatural" consciousness, we have no need to appeal to miracles, mysticism, or the subconscious. This awareness is available to any lucid person who strives to develop true beliefs (SRI, 271). Any group of people working together in the service of truth or good that transcends their individual consciousness become members of what Royce calls the "Invisible Church."

Royce understood the church in the ordinary use of the term, what he called the "Visible Church," to be an example of a community of believers in the higher unity of the spirit. Thus, by analogy, he extends the term "church" to apply to any community of believers in a higher unity. The invisible church is the "*community of all who seek salvation through loyalty* (SRI, 280). The unity remains "invisible" because of our narrowness and ignorance, and religious insight emerges as we become aware of the unity. The visible church is related to the invisible church as a part to the larger whole called "the unity of the spirit." Other visible manifestations of the higher unity include a community such as a business firm if its members are working together for a common good benefiting all people. We find the best example of the unity of the spirit in a community of scientists, even atheistic scientists, if genuinely loyal, who would shudder at the thought of being called a church.

To summarize Royce's position, we all naturally experience a need for salvation. We experience it first in the chaos of our individual lives and seek redemption in society. When we find that society itself remains chaotic, we seek salvation in reasonableness that reveals a superpersonal truth as the source of our salvation. We achieve salvation through loyalty, which we experience as both an act of will and as a gift of grace. The human experience of sorrow reveals both the need for salvation and the presently lost ideal that would bring salvation. We recognize as our supreme goal in life, the unity of the spirit exemplified in the community of the visible church but which in fact all communities of loyal persons embody when working for universally valid ideals such as scientific truth.

What James Missed

In specifying what James missed, this section will be restricted to a brief account of two of the seven sources. James had insight into the individual's sense of chaos and the need to overcome it. But because of his assumption that limits communal experience to the merely conventional, he did not discover social experience as a source of religious insight. In many of James's examples of the conversion experience, the person enters a dialogue with a being whom he identifies as God. The conversion can be motivated by a sense of guilt that means losing the connection with God. Royce, however, saw that a life-changing relationship can be found in a human face, and the sense of guilt can be expressed by being cut off from human society. If James had seen human society as a "variety of religious experience," it would have expanded and enriched his own vision. We can look at James's examples of solitary conversions based on inner dialogue as unusual examples of the dialogue that more often takes place between humans.

James's antirationalist outlook and his scorn for abstraction did not allow him to see reason as a source of insight. Reason could only be shallow and secondary. As James expressed his position:

> The struggle seems to be that of a less articulate and more profound part of our nature to hold out, and keep itself standing, against the attempts of a more superficial and explicit or loquacious part, to suppress it. (Perry, 2:238)[3]

By contrast, Royce's understanding that the essence of reason lies not just in analyzing, but also in connecting many things into an integrated unity, allowed him to see reason as compatible with intuition. James's view of conversion, mysticism, and saintliness reveals his insight of a world larger and more integrated than it seems to ordinary consciousness. Royce, in calling the integration reason, asserts that it can be articulated and integrated with the rest of our human experience. James's view remains prearticulate, but moving in the direction that Royce would carry further.

James's portrayal of conversion, sainthood, and mysticism reveal *insights* in Royce's sense of the term. However, James had an inadequate insight into religion in general that manifested itself in "a certain blindness" to the communal aspect of religion, in his appeal to the subconscious, and in his inability to see the rational connections that constitute salvation. James's insight can be reframed as true but incomplete manifestations of religious insights in Royce's sense of the term.

Royce's *Sources of Religious Insight* exemplifies the same larger insight found in his metaphysics, his concept of the self, and his ethics. The governing insight in all of Royce's thinking is that the individual human being becomes more and more of an individual as he or she expands the self to approach to a unity with all of being.

Part III

Charles Sanders Peirce

Chapter 11

Peirce and the Origin
of Pragmatism

ovelist Walker Percy said of Charles Sanders Peirce, "Most people
have never heard of him, but they will."[1] Peirce secured a position
as one of the landmark philosophers in the history of philosophy
even though he could not secure a permanent position as a university professor. Today, he is known worldwide and studied for his contribu-
tions to logic, epistemology, philosophy of science, and semiotics or the
theory of signs. In the context of American philosophy and of this book,
Peirce stands out as the acknowledged father of pragmatism. He also developed a rich and integrated system of metaphysics, theology, and ethics.

Although Peirce was three years older than James, and sixteen years
older than Royce, I am presenting his view third. A good case can be made
for keeping the three in their biographical order since Peirce had profound
influence on James and Royce. Most importantly, James credits Peirce for the
founding of pragmatism and Royce's most mature work stands on his 1912
insight into Peirce's logic. The three developed a close relationship, commu-
nicated both personally and by a large correspondence, and mutually influenced each other. However, by the time Peirce died, Royce and James, the
two best known of a far-famed Harvard Faculty, had attained a large measure
of recognition nationally and internationally. Peirce remained relatively
unknown outside of a small group of philosophers, a group that included John
Dewey as well as Royce and James. Although he had published twelve thousand pages, he left behind eighty thousand pages of unpublished manuscript.
After Peirce's death, Royce took charge of rescuing this material and presented it to Harvard University. The publication began in the early 1930s
and continues. Peirce as the founder and leader of the whole pragmatist

movement could be placed first among the three philosophers treated in this work. But his role among the most important proponents of American thought involves work that transcends his influence on his and later generations of Pragmatists. His national and international influence emerged later than that of James and Royce, and continues to expand.[2]

The present account of Peirce's work begins with a look at the origin of pragmatism especially noting how Peirce influenced James and how he and James differed. Next it examines Peirce's own philosophical speculations on the meaning of the human person, speculations that he called his "guess at the riddle." The final chapter on Peirce presents an interpretation of his ethical writing.

Since several excellent biographical accounts of Peirce's life are available,[3] this chapter will present only a brief summary to give the context of Peirce's philosophical labors. Peirce was the son of Benjamin Peirce, a prominent Harvard professor of mathematics and astronomy. Charles Peirce inherited from his father not only an extraordinary intelligence and love of learning, but also a religious reverence for mathematics and the order of the universe. But in spite of the nobility of his thinking, Charles's early life was far from exemplary. He suffered from neuralgia for which he took opium, a commonly prescribed but addictive analgesic. The disease and the medication contributed to his being extremely ill-tempered and uncivil. Peirce seemed to have a knack for insulting people and being generally disagreeable. Further, he divorced his wife and then married the woman he was thought to be having an affair with. In the nineteenth century, this was not only unacceptable, but apparently unforgivable. Peirce's personal deficiencies included the inability to handle money. He spent his resources with reckless abandon always hoping that he had a moneymaking idea around the next corner. As a result, in his old age he found himself not only impoverished, but William James had to literally rescue him from starvation (Brent, 305).

In his later years, reflecting back on his life and education he wrote that his father taught him concentration of mind. "But as to moral self-control, he unfortunately presumed that I would inherit his own nobility of character, which was so far from being the case that for long years I suffered unspeakably being an excessively emotional fellow, from ignorance of how to go to work to acquire sovereignty over myself" (Menand, 160).

When Peirce developed his philosophical ethics he emphasized self-control as the essential characteristic of an ethical life, a characteristic that he regretted he had not practiced very well himself. Peirce was brutally honest in his self-assessment, a characteristic that would not have been found in a person who lacked an intense moral sense. Unfortunately, the intensity of his moral sense did not translate into effectiveness. Two key features of Peirce's life reveal the depth of character that did not fit his public image of a man lacking in character. First, when he married for the first time he converted from his father's Unitarianism to his wife's Episcopalian faith. He would maintain this faith and practice throughout his life. Second, in spite of his reputation for profligacy, he faithfully cared for his second wife through illness and poverty, and devoted himself to the philosophical work which he believed God had assigned to him. The fruit of his devotion and labor will constitute the remainder of this section.

Frustrated in his wish for an academic career, Peirce spent most of his professional life working for the Geological Survey doing experiments in gravitation. Later in life he would see his career as an advantage to his philosophical insights. Explaining why philosophy had not developed as well as other sciences, he attributed it to the fact that the scholars who developed philosophy came from theological seminaries and lacked a background in experimental activity. Peirce stepped up with his rich background in the type of experimental study that he found wanting in previous philosophers.

Peirce's Pragmatism

Charles Sanders Peirce is best known for his theory of pragmatism. James had popularized pragmatism but gave Peirce credit for inventing the term and the philosophy that it connotes. Peirce did not agree with James's pragmatism, as will be explained, but he acknowledged that they each took a major part in a large and significant movement and Peirce took pride in his role as the primary author. According to Peirce, pragmatism means a method for clarifying the meaning of ideas. We can discover the meaning of an idea by asking ourselves what practical consequences will follow if an idea is true. For example, if we say that a diamond is hard, we mean that it will scratch other substances, such as glass, without being scratched. The consequences of trying to scratch, crush, burn, dissolve, or change the diamond in any way, constitute the whole meaning of the idea that a diamond is hard.

According to William James, Peirce introduced pragmatism into philosophy in an 1878 article, "How to Make Our Ideas Clear." James wrote this in "What Pragmatism Means," Lecture Two of his 1908 book, *Pragmatism*. According to James, the idea lay dormant for twenty years until he, James, brought it forward in an address at the University of California in 1898. This section will first look at the key ideas in Peirce's "How to Make our Ideas Clear," next sketch the sources of the idea in Peirce's early background, and then consider Peirce's 1903 interpretation of Pragmatism, including his differences with James.

René Descartes' assertion that ideas may be held true with certainty if they are "clear and distinct" provides the context for Peirce's title, "How to

Make Our Ideas Clear."[4] Peirce argued that an idea may seem clear if it is familiar. Distinctness depends on having good definitions, and while definitions are desirable they do not yield any new knowledge or certainty of the truth of empirical propositions. Peirce argues that thought needs more than a sense of clarity; it also needs a method for making ideas clear. Once we have made an idea clear, then we can begin the task of determining its truth. The method that Peirce offers came to be known as the pragmatic method and the epistemology on which it depends is pragmatism.

Peirce rejected Descartes' method of doubt. We cannot doubt something, for the sake of method, that we do not doubt in fact. In a later essay, he would state as his rule "Dismiss make-believes." This refers to Descartes' method of doubting things, in the safety of his study, such things as the existence of the material world, which he did not doubt when he went out on the street. Peirce proposed that a philosophical investigation can begin from only one state of mind, namely, the state of mind in which we find ourselves when we begin. If any of us examines our state of mind at a given time, we find two kinds of thoughts; beliefs, and doubts. Peirce had presented the interaction of doubt and belief in an earlier essay "The Fixation of Belief" (CP, 358–387). At any time we may be aware of beliefs and doubts. Beliefs consist of states of mind in which we would make a statement; doubts are states in which we would ask a question. We experience a doubt as a sense of uneasiness and hesitation. Doubt serves as an irritant that causes us to appease it by answering a question and thereby fixing a belief and putting the mind to rest on that issue. A common example of a doubt would be arriving in an unfamiliar city and not being sure of the location of our destination address in relation to our present location. We overcome this doubt and fix a belief by getting the directions. Once we achieve a belief, we can take the necessary action to reach our destination. Peirce defines a belief subjectively as something of which we are aware and which appeases the doubt. Objectively, a belief is a rule of action. The whole purpose of thought consists in overcoming a doubt and attaining a belief. Peirce acknowledges that some people like to think about things or argue about them without caring to find a true belief, but he asserts that such dilettantism does not constitute thought.

The beliefs that we hold determine how we will act. If we believe, rightly or wrongly, that the building that we are trying to reach sits one block to our north, we will walk in that direction. We have beliefs about matters of fact, near and far. For example, we believe in the reality objects in front of us and we believe generally accepted historical statements. We also believe in relations of ideas such as that seven and five equal twelve. In addition to these we have many beliefs about science, politics, economics, religion, and so on. Some of our beliefs may be false since we are capable of error. To believe something means to *think* that it is true.

In addition to defining a belief as a state of mind in which a person would make a statement and the mind sits at rest regarding that particular issue, an essential characteristic of a belief consists of its being a habit. We identify a habit by the action to which it leads under particular circumstances. To discover the meaning of a belief we need to ask what action follows from it. "Under what conditions does the habit lead us to act, and what is the action to which it leads?" In other words, what stimulus causes us to act if we have this particular belief, and what sensible results follow the action? Peirce's pragmatism holds that we find the meaning of any idea in the tangible results of the action to which it leads.

Pragmatism answers the question implied in his article, "How to Make our Ideas Clear." Peirce maintained that philosophy, as one of its most important tasks, serves to make our ideas clear. We make an idea clear by determining the consequences that will follow if the idea holds true. We discover the meaning of an idea by posing this question. Assume that the idea is true. What practical consequences will follow from its being true? If the idea has no consequences, then we cannot call it true or false; the idea is simply meaningless.[5]

Peirce gives a pragmatic explanation of reality itself. He begins with a common sense definition. We distinguish reality from fiction by defining the real as "that whose characters are independent of what anyone thinks them to be." To make the idea clear, Peirce applies the pragmatic rule. The meaning of anything consists in the sensible effects which it produces. When we apply this rule to the meaning of reality, we determine that the sensible effect of any real thing is to produce a belief. We must then distinguish between a true and a false belief. Peirce defines truth as that which if acted on, leads us to the point at which we aim and not astray. A reciprocal relationship holds between truth and reality. We understand reality as that which exists independently of the mind and which causes a belief or habit of action. We call a belief true if the action that it produces leads us to what we expect in reality. The scientific method serves to distinguish true from false beliefs. Peirce believed that if scientific research were pushed far enough on any problem, it would yield a solution on which all investigators would agree. He defined truth as the opinion on which all investigators are destined to agree. The object of that opinion is reality.

A seemingly paradoxical relationship develops between Peirce's method, which appears to be nominalistic and individualistic, and the above definition of reality, which characterizes truth as objective and social. The relationship between Peirce's pragmatism and his antinominalism can be seen in his early thinking.[6] Several notable young intellectuals formed a study group called "The Metaphysical Club" out of which came Peirce's term, "pragmatism." Several members advance the theme that legal terms such as "chain of causation" and "remote and proximate cause" do not refer to fixed entities, but rather the courts constructed them for practical reasons. Further, Darwin's *The Origin of Species* showed that unlike Aristotle's notion of eternally fixed forms, species stood for convenient ways to classify groups of living things. Peirce had come to the conclusion that even physical laws consist of approximations.

Nicholas St. John Green, a member of the Metaphysical Club, developed a pragmatic theory in a legal context and argued that the truth-value of legal concepts consists of their usefulness in sorting out and classifying otherwise unrelated legal situations. No two cases are exactly alike, but legal terms such as classifying a given type of violation of a contract or of a law, enable lawyers, judges, and juries to deal with cases, using a manageable number of principles.

The pragmatic theory of knowledge holds that knowers do not relate to objects as spectators who try to make their knowledge mirror whatever is given, but rather knowledge purposefully constructs a worldview in which we can act. This does not of course mean that we mold the facts to fit anything that we like. Our beliefs must be true for our actions to be successful.

One of the sources of Peirce's theory of knowledge, hence of pragmatism itself, was the Scottish philosopher Alexander Bain. Bain introduced the belief-doubt dynamic to the Metaphysical Club. Bain had defined a belief as that thought upon which we are prepared to act. Peirce had also been influenced by Chauncy Wright's naturalism, which sought continuity between animal instinct and human intelligence. Bain's description of belief contributes to making the animal-human connection. Bain described a belief as "...a primitive disposition to follow out any sequence that has been once experienced, and to expect the result."[7] The beliefs that we humans hold enable us to find our way through life analogously to the way that an animal's learned behavior does for that animal. Peirce applied the term "pragmatism" to the method of finding the meaning of a belief in the action that the person who holds the belief prepares to take.

Peirce's Critique of Nominalistic Pragmatism

Peirce sought to avoid two problems with his pragmatic interpretation of ideas. First he rejected the notion that the meaning and truth value of an idea can be restricted to the idea's usefulness in isolation from other truths and realities. Second, he did not want to limit the meaning of ideas to each individual's attempt to make his or her way through life. Peirce attempted to avert these problems by seeing pragmatism as a method within a larger philosophy rather than as a complete and self-contained philosophy (Apel, 58).

Peirce combated the philosophical view called "nominalism," the belief that only individuals are real. According to nominalism, general ideas merely constitute "names," hence the term "nominalism." This man or woman, or dog, or stone, is real, but the term "human" or "dog" or "stone" as applied to a whole class of things does not refer to anything real. Such terms serve as convenient tools to lump together things that bear similarity according to some useful criteria, but each in itself is fundamentally unique. The metaphysical view of nominalism seems to flow logically from the method of pragmatism as it in fact does in James's philosophy. But Peirce found nominalism unacceptable and rejected it in favor of what he called "scholastic realism."

Peirce, influenced by his astronomer father, Benjamin Peirce, believed that the world was made to be known by the human mind and that "the two are wonderfully matched" (Menand, 228). The mind thinks in general ideas and so true ideas must have a real object to which they refer. The whole process of human evolution involves the development of more and more general ideas. This process of generalization constitutes the whole meaning of moral development of which scientific endeavor is an exemplary instance. Chapter 13, which deals with Peirce's ethics, explains the process of development through generalization.

Along with his belief that true ideas are not limited to knowledge of individual things, Peirce argued that truths are not the exclusive property of each individual thinker. Nominalism would deny the reality of the social aspect of human beings both as knowers and as objects of knowledge. If the nominalists are right, reality consists of unique self-contained minds knowing unique events and communicating through fictions of general names. Peirce maintained the realist position that the object of true beliefs really subsists independently of any mind, and that science consists of a communal effort to get closer to true opinions of reality. The final result of any investigation, the opinion upon which the investigators are destined to agree, constitutes the true opinion. Reality is the ultimate object of the communal investigation.

Peirce did not use the term "pragmatism" in the 1878 article "How to Make Our Ideas Clear," the article that James cited as the beginning of pragmatism. In the twenty years between that article and James's acknowledgment in an 1898 article, Peirce had not used the term. While Peirce proudly accepted fatherhood of pragmatism, his own understanding of it had grown in a direction very different from that of James and other pragmatists. To mark the distinction, Peirce coined the term "pragmaticism," a term that he describes as so ugly it would remain safe from those who kidnapped "pragmatism."

We find a key difference in the way that James and Peirce understood pragmatism by looking at the context in which each of them used it. James made pragmatism a method, a theory of knowledge and truth including science, and a philosophy of human existence including an approach to our ultimate destiny. Peirce defined pragmatism as a method for clarifying ideas within a larger philosophical structure. The content of Peirce's philosophy will be presented in the following two chapters on the Human Person and on Ethics. However, a brief account of the context of pragmatism or pragmaticism in Peirce's thought might help at this point.

Two distinctions should be made at the outset. First, Peirce's Pragmatism did not deal with life's practical problems; Peirce never called his method "Practicalism." Second, his pragmatism did not stand alone either as a method of finding the meaning of ideas or of their truth. Rather he embedded it in a massive structure of thought which, following Immanuel Kant, Peirce called an architectonic. One part of that method consisted of clarifying ideas. In "How to Make Our Ideas Clear," he stated the first three of four degrees of clarity. Descartes cited clarity and distinctness as sufficient for certainty. Peirce argued that what Descartes called clarity was really familiarity. Any familiar idea may seem to be clear. But such apparent clarity may be illusory, and so while familiarity is necessary for conceptual clarity, it is not sufficient. The second of Descartes' terms, distinctness, refers to definition. Although a definition is also necessary for clarity, it does not give us any information beyond our present subjective awareness. The pragmatic method, which asks what action follows if a person believes the idea to be true, provides the third degree of clarity. For Peirce, action does not constitute the purpose of philosophical thought, but understanding the resulting action enables us to know what an idea means. The ultimate purpose of thought is to subsume ideas into greater and greater generalizations so that we achieve the most rational view of reality. Placing ideas in the most general, hence the most rational context, constitutes the fourth degree of clarity. The following chapter presents Peirce's method and insight regarding the human person.

Chapter 12

Charles Sanders Peirce on the Human Person

Charles Sanders Peirce asserted that the individual self, apart from other selves is an illusion. The notion that the separate self is an illusion runs contrary to the individualism that has governed modern Western thought from before the time of John Locke to the present. Political democracy and the system of capitalism and private ownership developed on the assumption that the individual first subsists, and then enters into arrangements with other individuals for their mutual benefit. The preeminence that each of us bestows on our separate selves bolsters the belief in the reality of separate individuals. Each of us seems to be self-contained and self-centered, and our cooperation and communication take place among ready-made selves. If Peirce stands correct and the separate self is an illusion, it certainly stands out as a powerful and attractive illusion and must have a basis in reality. To understand what Peirce meant by the self, we must probe his reasons for considering the separate self to be an illusion, as well as the basis in reality for the illusion. The idea of the self can be understood in the context of Peirce's major metaphysical premises, which the following paragraphs will try to make clear.

Peirce's Critique of the Separated Self

Peirce based his rejection of the self as a separate entity on his rejection of nominalism, the belief in irreducible unknowable entities. The nominalism of Peirce's time stemmed from seventeenth-century British empiricism as initiated and developed by Locke, Berkeley, and Hume. According to nominalistic empiricism, each idea consists of an isolated experience, whether a perception such as this or that tree, or a concept such as the abstract notion of a tree. The word "tree" in each case represents just the *name* or label of a particular concrete experience. The nominalists admit of no universal tree of which the particular trees serve as instances. Each of the experiences stands alone until the mind connects them through association. The experience of one object might resemble the experience of another, so we call them by the same name, for example "tree." According to Locke and Berkeley, each self knows only it own ideas. Hume carried the notion of nominalism further and argued that what we name as a "self" consists only of a bundle of perceptions.

Peirce, by contrast, held that no idea stands isolated from others. Each idea is signified by some things and in turn signifies others. Peirce called the continuity that exists among all things and ideas, *synechism,* a word he coined from the Greek word for continuity. Synechism serves as one of Peirce's fundamental metaphysical beliefs. According to the theory of synechism, all phenomena consist of the same character and differ only in degree. Mind and body lie on a continuum. Some realities are more material and regular; others more spiritual and spontaneous. The embodied human self exists in communion with other selves, and only in illusion does the self exist separately from other embodied selves. According to this view, I do not completely constitute myself; my neighbor, to some extent *is* myself, and I *am* my neighbor's self. This view will probably seem disturbing if not down right absurd to an individualist. Further elaboration will hopefully clarify and justify the theory.

According to Peirce's theory, each of us consists of a cell in a social organism. Before any other characteristic, our particular array of faults and limitations distinguishes us, as individuals, from the social organism. Such a one-sidedly negative view of individualism may have reflected Peirce's own lifelong struggle to be accepted.[1] But common childhood experience reminds us that we most easily call attention to ourselves by being out of step with social expectations. We base our strong lifelong sense of individualism on our blind will, a force on the organic level that falls below the level of personhood. Each organism naturally inclines to give top priority to its own survival. Human personhood, however, has the capacity for much more and can achieve self-control and live in community with other selves. The capacity for self-control presents a puzzle. If the self is an illusion how can it develop self-control? Moreover, how can the self enter into community with other selves who are themselves presumably illusions? This question provokes the more basic question dealing with how the self emerges and of what it consists.[2]

The strong sense of the self, as distinct or even separate from others, rests on the reality that each of us is embodied in an organism. The importance of the organism to itself along with the special features of the human organism explains how a child develops its own self-consciousness. The human organism experiences itself as sentient, active, communicative, and cognitive. These characteristics make it conscious of the world in which it lives. But we derive self-consciousness from interacting with other minds. The child perceives itself as being distinct from others by being aware of the differences in perception between itself and other people. This mostly occurs as a result of errors on the part of the child. For example, if parents tell the child that the stove is hot, he might not believe it until he learns from a painful experience. Then he discovers the error of his own judgment and the truth of the words that the adults expressed.

The child therefore discovers itself through communication with others. The self is *distinct* from others but does not exist separately from them. To be a self means to be at least a potential member of a community (CP, 5:402). We *discover* ourselves through our own ignorance and error, but ignorance and error do not *constitute* the self. We err if we think of the self as a separate entity, but not if we think that the self is distinct. An aspect of the self stands out as unique. According to Vincent Colapietro:

> The self is truly something unique and irreducible in itself, but what it is in itself is only revealed or, more accurately, realized through its relation to others. It should be noted that these others need not be present or even actual. The others to whom a self is principally related may not yet exist. (Colapietro, 74)

Colapietro observes that Peirce, who worked in solitude, wrote primarily for those who would come after him. A distinct and ineffable aspect of each self, while real, does not constitute the entirety or essence of the self. The self is realized and revealed in its communication with others.

Since the self not only reveals, but also realizes itself only in the company of others, there must be another for the self to communicate with in order to become a self. The essential role of communication manifests what Peirce called the "General Law of the Mind." According to the General Law of the Mind: "Ideas tend to spread continuously and to affect certain others which stand to them in a peculiar relation of affectability" (CP, 6:104). Mental phenomena tend to move toward greater and greater integration, and complexity, and to form larger syntheses. This law explains the development of personality. For example, as we develop from childhood toward adulthood, our various and sometimes conflicting feelings, thoughts, and desires become more integrated to form a sense of personal identity.

The self remains always in dialogue. When engaged in solitary thinking, it talks to itself. The self consists of a process and the existing aspect talks to the aspect that is coming into existence. The intrapersonal dialogue in turn potentially takes part in a larger dialogue, which the person carries on within the various communities in which he or she participates. These communities are not mere collectives, but have a personal reality of their own. Therefore, according to Peirce, within the human organism, there are selves whose dialogue constitutes the self in the ordinary sense of an individual human person, and the persons carry out a dialogue that constitutes a larger self. Thinking involves dialogue, and a community involved in the dialogue of several individuals takes on a trans-individual personal status. The self cannot be understood as an entity apart from other selves and apart from its future and the future of other selves. According to Peirce's "synechism," no absolute gap yawns between one self and another. The idea of synechism even implies that selves in communion with one another form a higher self. This communal idea of the self will be developed further in the next chapter on Peirce's ethical theory.

We find a key to understanding Peirce's account of the self in his assertion that the self is essentially a sign. A sign is anything that represents something to a mind. Any time we think, we are conscious of some representation, which serves as a sign. It may be a concept, an image, or even a feeling. Peirce understood language as a system of signs and the self as the sum total of a person's language.

Identifying ourselves with a system of signs presents a difficulty because we each tend to identify ourselves with our will. Peirce describes the will as the power that we have over our animal organism, the power to move it by brute force. Or perhaps we identify ourselves with the whole biological organism. This identification constitutes the psychological origin of selfishness, and rests on our natural inclination to give priority to our biological survival. Each organism tends to treat itself as of primary importance. But Peirce considers the organism to be only an instrument of thought. The thinking mind requires a body since every thought consists of a symbol, and all symbols must be embodied.

The human personality does not exist as a discrete and separate being, but rather as a continuous being. It cannot be formed or apprehended in an instant since it develops in time. The personality cannot reach its fullest development in any finite period of time; at each finite instant of time it lives in the present, although not completely. Since personality is by its very nature temporal, it remains forever incomplete and essentially unrealizable. Because we exist finitely, no person ever fully actualizes who he or she is. In the course of our lives, we each become partially realized, but to a greater extent, remain unrealized. This inability to realize ourselves constitutes the tragic aspect of human existence and the reason that, in Colapietro's words, "...death is *always* tragic" (Colapietro, 76).

The emphasis on the unrealizability of the self indicates a teleological view of the self. The self consists of a teleological harmony of ideas. The personality does not have explicit and fixed ends. If the ends were already determined, the development of the personality would be mechanical and therefore not personal. The personality must be flexible in its orientation to the future. Its teleology consists of its natural tendency toward ever-greater differentiation and integration. But since interpreting signs remains an ongoing process, and each interpretation in turn becomes a sign that can be interpreted, the personality itself is always new and always unfinished.

The Illusory Self and the Authentic Self

Because Peirce identifies the basic characteristic of the mind, the law of the mind, as continuity, the mind of one person cannot be a private sphere separated from its fellows by an unbridgeable chasm. Rather, the mind is a communicative agent with the ability to overcome the separateness which is characteristic of the willful organism's sense of self-supremacy. The self remains somewhat imprisoned in its sphere of solitude because of its cognitive and affective limitations. It follows that overcoming its limitations through cognitive and affective growth, that is, growth in understanding and love constitutes the developmental task of any self. The solitary self remains illusory with its roots in selfishness. The authentic self is communicative and has its roots in agape.

The ideal of reasonableness requires the ability to be open to that which confronts the self. We may perceive another person or an inner thought as foreign. The idea of other, serves as the very pivot of thought. The ideal of reasonableness runs contrary to the natural tendency to run away from or to destroy what we consider foreign. We naturally perceive the foreign as a hated enemy. In the effort to overcome natural hostility, an intimate connection between reasonableness and love emerges. That is why Peirce argues that reason is "agapaistic," a term he coined from *agape*, love. As Peirce puts it: "Love, recognizing germs of loveliness in the hateful, gradually warms it to life, and makes it lovely" (CP, 6:289). Colapietro makes an analogy between the work of love and that of reason: "Reason as a form of love, seeing germs of reasonableness in the irrational, gradually warms it into life and makes it rational. What love is in the affective domain, reason is in the cognitive sphere—namely, a creative process of generalization" (Colapietro, 92).

Thinking consists of a dialogue between different phases of the ego and constitutes a wave on the surface of the soul. But although the dialogue remains superficial, it has a real effect. Through a gradual process the eternal forms, expressed in rational dialogue, will reach the deepest parts of our soul and influence our lives. The eternal forms constitute the ideals that are part of the eternal growth of reasonableness.

Our commitment to ideals consists of a series of acts of surrender. Our ideals take possession of us rather than we taking possession of them. The realization of the self requires the surrender to more and more inclusive ideals. The self-centered self remains lawless and illusory. The self-transcendent self requires the surrender of egoism, and constitutes self-possession. Through self-surrender to ideals we find the meaning of our existence. Peirce ranks the continuous growth of reasonableness as the only admirable ideal. The embodiment of this ideal constitutes the purpose of our life. We can achieve this ideal in artistic creation, in useful work, and above all, in theoretical constructions. We do not constitute the absolute source of our actions. We are signs by which absolute beauty is brought into contact with brute existence (Colapietro, 96–97). The following chapter on ethics presents the human purpose of embodying the ideal.

Chapter 13

Ethics and the Purpose
of Human Life

Peirce maintained that while philosophical ethics can be a legitimate
pursuit, it cannot and should not try to deal with issues of vital
importance. He made a clear distinction between practical and theoretical ethics. Practical ethics should not deal with questions such
as *why* we should be beneficent, honest, truthful, loyal. Theoretical ethics
deals with these questions, but its investigations are not useful in trying to
teach people, especially young people how to live their lives. Practical ethics
has *vital importance*, but it cannot be scientific and should not pretend to be.
Scientific ethics, in turn, has no value for vital interest. These two disci-
plines should not be confused; when we confuse them we spoil both. I propose here to give an account of Peirce's ethics and argue within a Peircean
perspective, that ethics can deal with vital interests scientifically, and then
show how Peirce's philosophical ethics can serve as the basis for a contemporary virtue ethic.

This section first presents Peirce's argument against the practicality of
ethics; next it presents a description of his architectonic, showing the place of
ethics. The central part is an analysis of Peirce's notion of the *summum
bonum*, concrete reasonableness to show the reconciliation between theory
and his practice. The conclusion consists of an outline of a foundation for a
Peircean virtue ethic.

Reasons for the Incompatibility of Practical and Theoretical Ethics

A reading of Peirce's description of ethics will likely dishearten anyone
interested in philosophical ethics. Peirce made a distinction between theoret-

ical science and vital interests. He insisted that the former be disinterested and therefore not attempt to be practical. The pursuit of vital interests, by contrast, must avoid the hypocrisy of pretending to be scientific. Vital interests, by definition, pertain to this or that individual life, but in the whole scheme of things vital interests are relatively insignificant. Clergy, teachers, and all those who study ethics as a way of guiding their own lives, or the lives of others, must rely on tradition and instinct. Philosophers, in turn, who investigate the meaning of the good, must do so objectively and disinterestedly and never pretend that their investigations can be of vital importance in guiding anyone's life. Furthermore, no one can serve two masters by pursuing ethics as theory and as practice. Peirce bluntly tells his readers that he has no "philosophical wares that will make them better or more successful" (CP, 1.621).

Peirce defined the ideal of practical *ethics* as " . . . nothing but a sort of composite photograph of the conscience of the members of the community. In short it is nothing but the traditional standard, accepted, very wisely, without radical criticism, but with a silly pretense of critical examination" (CP, 1.573). The science of ethics, in this view, consists of nothing more than the study of what today, following Lawrence Kohlberg, might be called "conventional morality." Or it could be described in the words of Peirce's contemporary, William Graham Sumner, as the *mores* of the society. This kind of ethics, in the hands of clergy, teachers, and parents can be useful, but not scientific. Those philosophers, who think that they study this discipline critically, and that they base their conclusions on well-examined theory, simply delude themselves.

Peirce described, as a task of practical ethics, a series of self-criticisms that all morally serious people must undertake to make sure that their conduct conforms to their ideals. A moral action begins with a general intention that conforms to and promotes the person's ideals. In a particular case, the person may make a resolution in keeping with the intention. After the fact the first act of self-criticism requires the person to reflect on whether the conduct remained true to the resolution. The second question asks whether the conduct accords with the general intention, and finally whether the intention itself conforms to the person's ideals. A further and deeper meditation is to examine the ideals themselves to judge their fitness for the particular person. At each step a feeling of pleasure or pain accompanies the examination and reveals the fitness or lack of fitness (CP, 1.594–1.599). (Peirce, of course, was not a hedonist. We do not live for pleasure, but pleasure and pain can serve as a symptom of fitness or lack thereof.) But beyond this practical self-examination, the student of theoretical ethics may ask, "as a matter of curiosity," what constitutes the *fitness* of an ideal. In case the reference to "curiosity" does not seem demeaning enough to dampen the zeal of theoretical ethicists, Peirce adds the following sentence that will surely get their attention. "Opinion differs as to the wholesomeness of this study." He pointedly distinguished ethical theory from the practical task of shaping one's conduct. But he concluded on a faintly positive note. As long as the distinction between theory and practice is kept in mind, theoretical ethics is "more or less favorable to right living" (CP, 1.600).

Scientific and practical thought differ essentially in their pursuit and progress. Science fulfills its purpose in discovering ideal eternal truths. If scientists try to use science to further their own or others' vital interests, the investigation becomes biased and fails as science. Since philosophy is a branch of science, it too must remain disinterested and unattached to vital interests. The need to separate science from vital interests rests on the distinction between beliefs and opinions. Beliefs are states of mind that we act on, and include not only the common sense beliefs that control our everyday conduct, but also our deepest ethical and religious beliefs. But neither our common sense nor our deepest beliefs depend on reason. In Peirce's analogy, if you hear your sister in danger and calling for help, you do not begin to reason out what it means for one person to hear another person's call. No, you respond immediately. Likewise, if you encounter a religious experience that you interpret as the call of your Savior, you respond with action rather than with theological reasoning. A scientific hypothesis by contrast, is an opinion. You hold it only tentatively and act on it only in the sense of testing it experimentally. You readily let go of it if the experiment falsifies it. To hold on to it as a belief would spoil science, just as a tentative opinion about vital matters would spoil your ability to act on them.

Theoretical ethics, as a branch of philosophy, therefore cannot act in the service of practical interests. Peirce reminded his readers that no one can serve two masters. Ethics can be practical or theoretical but not both. Practical ethics depends on sentiment and tradition; theoretical ethics must be based on logic. Peirce contended that philosophy, of which theoretical ethics constitutes a part, remains in its infancy after two thousand years. He attributed this retardation to the fact that most philosophers lack training in the method of scientific investigation, the kind of training that marked Peirce's own life and work. Furthermore, even if philosophy were developed, there would be scarcely any people who possess reasoning powers sharp enough to master it. Most people tend to exaggerate their logical powers, yet lack of first class reasoning power does not prevent people from living good and successful lives. The deficiency that most people have in reasoning proficiency makes no important difference as they pursue their vital interests. As Peirce summed up the common lack of reasoning power:

> We all know highly successful men, lawyers, editors, scientific men—not to speak of artists—whose great deficiency in this regard is only revealed by some unforeseen accident. (CP, 1.657)

What of those few in the population who master higher mathematics? Peirce says that their interests, as mathematicians, scientists, and philosophers are not *vital*, that is, it does not concern theirs or others' individual lives. Peirce identified mathematicians, specifically modern mathematicians, as Platonists concerned with eternal forms. He based this observation on conversations with mathematicians and, of course, he spoke from firsthand experience as a scientist, logician, and philosopher. What does concern the mathematician?

> The eternal is for him a world, a cosmos, in which the universe of actual existence is nothing but an arbitrary locus. The end that pure mathematics is pursuing is to discover that real potential world. (CP, 1.646)

The person who is drawn to such goals finds the vital interests of humans to be of little importance. After describing what the mathematician lives for and admires he warns:

> But such ideas are only suitable to regulate another life than this. Here we are in this workaday world, little creatures, mere cells in a social organism, itself a poor and little thing enough and we must look to see what little and definite task our circumstances have set before our little strength to do. The performance of that task will require us to draw upon all of our powers, reason included, and in the doing of it we will depend not upon that department of the soul which is most superficial and fallible—I mean our reason—but upon that department that is deep and sure—which is instinct. (CP, 1.647)

Peirce did, however, attempt to build a bridge between the development of higher mathematical reasoning and the daily duties of humans. In his philosophy of Synechism, the superficial rational part of the soul cannot be discontinuous with the deeper instinctive part. Reason can have a part to play in the development of instinct because the deeper part can be reached only through the superficial part.

> In this way, the eternal forms that mathematics and philosophy and the other sciences make us acquainted with, will by slow percolation gradually reach the very core of one's being; and will come to influence our lives; and this they will do, not because they involve truths of merely vital importance, but because they are ideal and eternal verities. (CP, 1.648)

To sum up this argument, theoretical reasoning and practical ethics must be kept distinct. Reason lacks the capability of governing our vital interests and instinct does it much better. If we place science, including philosophy, in the service of our vital interests, we spoil both. Science must remain disinterested so it can fulfill its function of discovering eternal truths. If it does so, it can slowly help instincts to grow and thereby to have a positive influence on our daily lives. With this in mind, I will proceed to show how Peirce's philosophy might have this indirect effect on our attempts to grow ethically and morally.

The Place of Ethics in Peirce's Architectonic

In his classification of the normative sciences, Peirce stated that "esthetics, practics, and logic form one distinctly marked whole." (By *practics*, he meant what is generally called ethics. Except in direct quotations, or in contexts where Peirce's distinctions are relevant, this work will use the term "ethics" to refer to the science of correct actions.) The distinction between these sciences ranks secondary to their unity. "Esthetics relates to feeling, practics to action, and logic to thought" (CP, 1.457). In building his architectonic, Peirce placed logic subordinate to ethics, since logic consists of nothing more than correct practice in the area of thought. Ethics in turn is subordinate to esthetics, because ethics needs to find the *summum bonum*, which we know through esthetics. This idea requires some explanation.

Peirce showed a close parallel between ethically good conduct and correct logical reasoning. A series of criticisms brings the essential character of logic and ethics under self-control. He writes:

> The phenomena of reasoning are, in their general features, parallel to those of moral conduct. For reasoning is essentially thought that is under self-control, just as moral conduct is conduct under self-control. (CP, 1.606)

In the case of moral conduct, we begin with conduct that *seems* to be right, based on instinct and tradition. This conduct, if inconsistent, falls under criticism by ourselves and others. We then face the obligation to modify our conduct to keep it consistent with our ideals. In logical reasoning, we begin with a conjecture that seems to be true. We criticize it to see if it holds consistent with other propositions that we take to be true. Deductive reasoning plays this role. Biographer Joseph Brent argues that "(t)here is nothing in this view to prevent us from being constant liars, consistent adulterers, or persistent cads" (Brent, 343.) However, in the case of moral conduct, in addition to being consistent, we need to look at what the effect would be if we carry out the conduct. Obviously, harmful conduct is not good even if it is logically consistent with an ideal. Peirce demonstrated the parallel between conduct and reason in each of the three steps of his logical method. The conjecture must seem true and the conduct fine. We then use deductive reasoning to show the consistency of the conduct as well as the reasoning. Finally, "certain ways of reasoning recommend themselves because if persistently carried out they must lead to truth." And so, after self-criticism to make sure our conduct remains consistent with our ideals, "we consider what the general effect would be of thoroughly carrying out our ideals" (CP, 1.608). Much as the logicians or scientists must see what happens if they follow their line of reasoning, so the person making an ethical decision must examine the full implications of his or her choice. Discerning the consequences of an action is analogous to the role of experiment in science. Therefore, the parallel between logic and ethics is, in Peirce's estimation, perfect.

How does esthetics fit into this architectonic? Ethics depends on esthetics just as logic depends on ethics. Right ethical reasoning can be defined as reasoning that is conducive to our ultimate good. The logician needs the ethicist (Peirce uses the term *moralist*) to define the ultimate end. The ethicist only knows the ultimate end as whatever is admirable in itself without any other reasons. Esthetics has the task of defining the admirable in itself (CP, 1. 611). Peirce calls it the *beautiful*, but does not allow this to be an answer to the question of what constitutes the admirable. The task of analysis must be to find the characteristics of that which is the most admirable— admirable in itself. Peirce takes it as evident that it must be an ideal, and as such it must be general. No particular thing and certainly no particular subjective feeling can be the most admirable ideal. Peirce's notion of an ideal implies that it must be not only general, but also unified. We might identify several admirable ideals, but there must be some character that constitutes the unity of the admirable itself, some quality that characterizes all admirable ideas.

In describing the meaning of the most admirable ideal, Peirce gives an analysis of reason itself. He uses the terms *reason, ideas, and general,* almost interchangeably. He identifies *Reason* as the process of *generalization* that manifests itself in nature and in the human mind. The human faculty of *reason* is a manifestation of the *general* process of the evolution of the universe. The term *idea* refers to this or that particular manifestation of *generalization*. Manifestations are individual events included in a general idea. Peirce states twice within eleven lines that "The very being of Reason, of the General, *consists* in governing individual events (CP, 1.615). This statement reveals two momentous implications. First, an idea must be embodied in order to be fulfilled. Second, an idea can never be completely fulfilled, but remains always incipient and growing. We can always make potential or hypothetical predictions from an idea. Ideas possess more possible manifestations than anyone can ever realize. Peirce drew the parallel with the character of a human person. Character consists of the ideas that persons will conceive and the effort they will make if the occasion calls for it. But persons can never manifest all of their ideals and the possible actions that would serve them; they can never realize all of their potential. The character of a person is a general idea, and like every general idea, its full manifestation would require more individual events than can ever occur. Life remains always dynamic and death is always tragic because there always remains more to do for fulfillment.

Through this discussion Peirce has brought us to the definition of the admirable in itself and to the ethical and logical implications.

> The development of Reason consists, you will observe, in embodiment, that is, in manifestation. The creation of the universe, which did not take place during a certain busy week in the year 4004 B.C., but is going on today and never will be done, is this very development of Reason. I do not see how one can have a more satisfying ideal of the admirable than the development of Reason so understood. (CP, 1.615)

So stands the goal of esthetics, to describe the admirable, which Peirce has identified as the development of reason. Ethics has as its goal to bring human conduct into service of such an ideal as the ultimate good.

> Under this conception the ideal of conduct will be to execute our little function in the operation of the creation by giving a hand toward rendering the world more reasonable whenever, as the slang is, it is "up to us." (CP, 1.615)

The task of scientific ethics is to discover what it takes to embody the ideal. In carrying the Peircean ideal beyond Peirce, ethicists will ask disinterestedly what practical women and men can do to make the world more reasonable when it is "up to them." How can actions in areas such as business, technology, health care, law, and education embody the ideal of reasonableness? Logic helps ethics work toward the ideal by teaching the methods that develop reasonableness most speedily. Following Peirce's method, ethicists first guess at what would be the best course. Their next step requires a careful and honest deduction of the implications of their guess. Finally, they critically examine the results of actions which follow from the implications of their hypothesis. Self-criticism serves to determine whether their ethical assertions do or do not contribute to the ideal of reasonableness.

This can be illustrated by using a case that Peirce described. In reviewing a book on ethics, Peirce cited an example that the author used.

> A judge, let us suppose, has brought before him a case in which a man suffers injury for which he claims damages of another. "Take," he says, " the

case where A's cattle break out of their enclosure in spite of A's having used all the care he reasonably could have used, or could learn to use, and destroy B's valuable crop in an adjoining field." (CP, 8.159)

Peirce ridiculed the author, a professor Mezes, for basing his ethical analysis on the scholastic notion of proximate cause. Peirce believed that such an idea has nothing to do with why the judge makes a decision, nor should it. Peirce thought instead that the right ethical decision can be made based on common sense, and so gives us an example to illustrate and test his notion of ethical thinking:

> . . . the real reason why the judge awards damages to B is that to allow a private person to undertake business humanly sure in the long run to injure his neighbors (and all the more so if he cannot learn to use suitable preventive measure), and then to allow him to pocket all the profits, and make his neighbors pay for incidental losses, would be to bring himself and his court into public contempt and into no little danger. (CP, 8.160)

Peirce saw that, in this case, a threat to the neighbors' crops constitutes part of the cost of raising cattle. The cattle rancher should pay this cost when it happens or carry an insurance policy that would cover it. This added expense would mean higher cost for the cattle rancher, but this constitutes part of his real cost and should not be born by the neighbor, except to the extent that the neighbor buys beef and shares the increased cost with every other consumer.

This case and its common sense solution, serves as an example of what Peirce described as conduct that seems to be right based on instinct and tradition. The next step involves a series of self-criticisms beginning with testing the idea for consistency. If we carry out a Peircean analysis of this example, we first look at the implications of our reasoning in this case to see if we could consistently follow it. A judge should not make a decision so obviously unfair that it would cause him to be held in public contempt. Peirce assumes that it is unfair for people to make a profit at the expense of others without compensating them. Would ethical people deliberately adopt a public policy that stipulated that anyone who conducted a business or industry or private activity that inevitably leads to harm to another should compensate the harmed parties for their loss, even if there is no negligence? The answer, I hold, is clearly yes. In the case that Peirce cited, the cattle rancher took all the precautions that he knew, or was capable of learning, to protect the neighboring farmers. What would this mean today for manufacturers who produce hazardous products or hazardous waste? A victim of an unavoidable accident ought not to bear the whole burden of a process in which others realize a profit. The persons whose activity caused the harm should assume the compensation as part of the expense of their activity. The result in the case of industry includes not only that innocent victims will be compensated, but that even the most insensitive of business executives will have a strong incentive to protect workers, consumers, and bystanders.

This analysis demonstrated how Peirce's common sense approach to ethics might work. Of course the whole edifice rests on what Peirce calls "sentiments" such as fairness and benevolence. The ethicist must assume these sentiments, but cannot produce them if they are missing. Without such sentiments, a person could ignore the fate of others, calculate the chance of being a victim himself, and be willing to take the risk for the sake of lower prices.

What can we conclude from the foregoing about the role of ethics? This will be treated in the final part of this chapter. But a short answer in the present context is in order. The virtues which philosophical ethics can help instill, include the habit of logical self-criticism so that we learn to apply logical principles consistently and thoroughly to the conclusions that our moral sentiments provide for us.

Peirce's architectonic shows the dependency and parallelism between logic and ethics. In scientific reasoning, we begin with a guess, draw out the implications by deductive reasoning and use experiment to see if the predicted results occur. So in ethics, we start with an assumption based on sentiment and tradition, use logic to deduce the implications of our maxim if it is consistently applied, and then estimate the consequences to determine the universal feasibility of our original principle. Peirce explained ethics by analogy to logic because the reasoning process is more familiar when expressed in logic than when applied to ethics. But logic stands subordinate to ethics because logic consists of right conduct applied to thought. We cannot think logically without the ethical commitment to truth and to the rigorous self-criticism necessary to approach truth. Finally, just as logic depends on ethics, so ethics depends on the science of the admirable in itself, aesthetics. Peirce defines the admirable in itself as the development of reason. The next part of this chapter will show what the ideal of reason meant to Peirce in terms of his notion of evolution and its social and ethical implications.

Love and Evolution

Peirce worked out a philosophical worldview comprehensive enough to include and integrate a physical and biological theory of evolution with the ethical teachings of Jesus (and the Buddha.) In fact, he saw science and ethics as aspects of the very same process. He expresses the process in his "The Law of the Mind," and bases it on his metaphysical theories of

Synechism, Tychism, and Agapism. The latter three terms mean that the reality is characterized by continuity, chance, and love. Each of these must be explained after a summary of what Peirce meant by his "Law of the Mind."

> ...there is but one law of mind, namely, that ideas tend to spread continuously and to affect certain others which stand to them in a peculiar relation of affectability. In this spreading they lose intensity, and especially the power of affecting others, but gain generality and become welded with other ideas. (CP, 6.104)

This process happens not only in the minds of humans, but also makes up the process of the universe itself. When Peirce referred to matter as an expression of mind, he clearly did not reduce matter to an illusory or unsubstantial mental phenomenon. He saw mind as the fundamental reality. Both the material world and what we ordinarily call mind, in the sense of human mental phenomena, are aspects of the same larger reality. So the spreading of ideas and their affecting others occurs in the human mind as we learn and acquire habits. But spreading of ideas also describes the physical evolution of the universe as matter grows in complexity and integration.

The term Synechism means that continuity among all ideas prevails. Every idea connects to some other idea so that, at least indirectly, all are connected to the whole. Tychism, from the Greek *tyche*—chance, means that the universe is not locked in a mechanical determinism. Instead room opens for real change and therefore for real growth. Not all change involves growth. Left to chance alone, things more likely fall apart. The power of *agape*—love makes evolutionary growth and development possible. Ideas may be forced together by mechanical necessity, which entails accumulation but not real growth, or they may fall apart by the disintegrating power of chance. But evolution occurs when they come together by an attraction toward real growth. The power of real growth makes physical and biological evolution as well as the social integration of human society possible.

Peirce argued that only love can produce growth. He illustrated this by the example of a creative human idea. Creative people see an idea as if it were a child. They nourish it as they would a flower in their garden. In so doing they enable the creation to reach its perfection. Peirce finds an example of evolutionary growth in the gospel command to love your neighbor, which means to ardently desire to fulfill your neighbor's highest impulse. The process of growth through attraction and integration provides the foundation of an evolutionary philosophy that explains the whole development of the universe.

> Love, recognizing germs of loveliness in the hateful, gradually warms it into life, and makes it lovely. (CP, 6.289)

In integrating evolution with ethics, Peirce offered a solution to the problem of evil. He attributed the solution to the elder Henry James who wrote that while it may be tolerable for us in our finite creaturely love to love others for their conformity to ourselves, the highest creative Love cares "for what is most bitterly hostile and negative to itself" (CP, 2.287). Peirce referred to the Gospel of John, which he saw as an early expression of an evolutionary philosophy. According to John's Gospel, God is Love. Peirce argues that hatred cannot be the contrary of the Love that is God, because if it were, then Satan would be coequal with God. Peirce understood evil as a defect as darkness is a defect of light. This, of course, expresses a traditional position in Christian philosophy, but Peirce integrated it into the whole of his evolutionary philosophy. Hatred and evil compose "mere imperfect stages of {*agape*} and {*agathon*}, love and loveliness" (CP, 6.287). Love limited to self-love, would be no love at all. God loved hatred and evil as imperfect stages of love. "Love your enemy," therefore, does not just express an ethical command (a seemingly irrational one), but represents the reason for the creation of the universe.

Peirce's view of evolution differs drastically from the then prevailing view of Darwin. Peirce described Darwin's view as tychistic, meaning that the prevailing force is not *agape*—love, but *tyche*—chance. In criticizing this view Peirce gave a scorching critique of the ethical values of his time. While acknowledging the strength of Darwin's argument for evolution by natural selection, Peirce contended that its wide reception did not result from its scientific validity. Writing twenty years after the publication of *The Origin of Species*, Peirce pointed out that Darwin's thesis had not yet been proven and seemed less hopeful than when it was first published.[1] Peirce attributed the acceptance of Darwin to the fact that his theory encouraged what Peirce called the "philosophy of greed." (Not that Darwin's own science was influenced by this philosophy.) If all higher life forms are dependent on a process of accidental variation, and survival depends on the self-interest of individual organisms, then we can justify a social and economic order that allows and even encourages individuals to seek their own self-interest. Such a policy, according to this political and economic theory, brings about progress whereas a policy based on "sentiment" leads to the degradation of the human race.

Peirce predicted that the nineteenth century would be remembered as the Economical Century. In describing the thought characteristic of the age he wrote:

> Well, political economy has its formula of redemption, too. It is this: Intelligence in the service of greed ensures the justest prices, the fairest contracts, the most enlightened conduct of all the dealings between men, and

leads to the *summum bonum*, food in plenty and perfect comfort. Food for whom? Why for the greedy master of intelligence. (CP, 6.290)

The economists, of course, did not include Peirce's final sarcastic sentence in their justification of self-interest, but argued that everyone fares better following self-interest than they would if they allowed "sentimentalism" to cloud their judgment. Peirce unabashedly defended sentimentalism. He pointed out that it received a bad name during the French Revolution, and that we generally associate it with either irrational violence or cheap dramatic performances. We disdain sentimentalism as an inability to think logically and an unwillingness to face facts. But as a doctrine, an "ism", sentimentalism means that "great respect should be paid to the natural judgments of the sensible heart." Peirce saw the scorning of sentiment as a blindness that would have terrible repercussions. He predicted that the economists will be shaken out of their complacency too late.

> The twentieth century, in its latter half, shall surely see the deluge-tempest burst upon the social order—to clear upon a world as deep in ruin as that greed-philosophy has long plunged it into guilt. (CP, 6: 292)

Peirce's prediction was wrong only in that the tempest-deluge came in the first half of the century.

Peirce based his evolutionary philosophy on a very different model than the Darwinian idea; Peirce argued that the driving force of evolution is love rather than chance. The ethical implications therefore differ greatly. Peirce summarized the difference between his view and Darwin's:

> The *Origin of Species* of Darwin merely extends the politico-economical views of progress to the entire realm of animal and vegetable life....As Darwin puts it on his title-page, it is the struggle for existence; and he should have added for his motto: Every individual for himself and the Devil take the hindmost! Jesus, in his Sermon on the Mount, expressed a different opinion (CP, 6.293)....Here then is the issue. The gospel of Christ says that progress comes from every individual merging his individuality in sympathy with his neighbors. On the other side, the conviction of the nineteenth century is that progress takes place by virtue of every individual's striving for himself with all his might and trampling his neighbor under foot whenever he gets a chance to do so. This may accurately be called the Gospel of Greed. (CP, 6. 294)

Peirce, in developing a theory of physical and biological evolution based on agape, provides a cosmic vision, integrated with both science and religion, that would justify a public policy and personal ethics that ran against the prevailing culture of his time.

Deriving a Virtue Ethic from Peirce's Theoretical Ethics

Peirce did not set out to create what we today call a "virtue ethics." The burden of teaching virtue falls on parents, teachers, and clergy. Virtue consists of the habit of living according to the principle of morality, which depends on instinct and culture, not science. Peirce places scientific ethics and moral virtue apart, but his principle of continuity seems to require that they be connected. The following paragraphs, while remaining faithful to Peirce's texts, offer an interpretation that will show how *we* can develop a virtue ethic enriched by Peirce's insights. It would be inappropriate to speak of "Peirce's virtue ethic," but we may advance a "Peircean" virtue ethic. This section attempts to show that Peirce's reasoning on deontological ethics provides "uberty," that it nourishes the ideals of truth, duty, and beauty by fostering virtue in those who understand his reasoning.

Virtue ethics involves the *habits* that govern everyday choices and actions. Theoretical ethics, including that of Peirce, provides right reasoning about normative principles and their application to problems. The two approaches need not exclude each other, although Peirce argues that the profession of the scientific ethicist and the teacher of morality must remain distinct.

Virtue ethics sometimes appears as a form of cultural relativism empty of universal norms. For example, although writers such as Aristotle and St. Thomas Aquinas attributed universal validity to their account of virtues, the relativists argue that these virtues apply only to ancient Athens and medieval Europe respectively.[2] Peirce proposed "concrete reasonableness" as a universal ideal. The virtues or habits that his ideas produce serve the universally admirable ideal. Reasonableness ranks as the highest and most general virtue, and it implies other habits, notably self-criticism and self-control. Making sense of a "Peircean virtue ethics" requires asking, how people would live their lives if Peirce's evolutionary metaphysics were their belief. This pragmatic question asks about the ethical implications of Peirce's philosophy. Following the pragmatic method, we can take Peirce's philosophy as a conjecture, a guess, and investigate the implications of its being true?[3] Would it lead to a consistent lifestyle producing consequences acceptable to our ethical instincts? The completion of such a study would take the form of an empirical examination of the expected conduct to evaluate it in terms of its movement toward or away from the ideal stated in the theory.

Working from Peirce's architectonic, we must first consider the aesthetic question of what is most admirable in itself? Peirce identifies the most admirable ideal as concrete reasonableness, which therefore stands as the *summum bonum* and the ultimate end of thought and action. Ethics serves as the study of the *behavior* that leads to the *summum bonum*, as logic studies the *thought* that leads to that end. Logical thought contributes to reasonableness, and therefore, people who dedicate themselves to any branch of science, mathematics, or philosophy engage in an ethically good activity. Peirce therefore rejected the notion that any science, including theoretical ethics, should be put in the service of vital interests. The pursuit of truth is good for its own sake and should not be contaminated by being subordinated to the vital interests of you or me.

Peirce believed, however, that the deeper part of the soul can be affected by the superficial cognitive part. Rational ideas can become beliefs and thereby affect our feeling and our action. Our reasoning affects our beliefs precisely by determining an ultimate end. As stated above, Peirce argued that the ultimate end is concrete reasonableness. He insisted that reasonableness be "concrete" because, far from armchair speculation, we must put reason to work in our individual and communal lives. To choose concrete reasonableness as an ultimate end does not betray the objectivity of science because it does not judge beforehand what constitutes reasonableness in any particular case. Belief in reasonableness stands in fact as a necessary condition for science. A belief is a habit that governs action and no one would do science if they did not believe in its worth. Therefore, belief in reasonableness presents itself as a goal that can be chosen and consistently acted on by the scientist, mathematician, and philosopher. We can ask whether this goal has anything to do with ethics besides the obvious ethical mandate of the scientific truth-seeker.

Belief in concrete reasonableness as an ultimate aim affects all of the actions of anyone who really believes it to be the ultimate aim. It leads those who hold it to act reasonably in every aspect of their lives. Belief in concrete reasonableness ordinarily does not produce a *sudden* conversion experience, but rather a slow process of habit formation.[4] Reasonableness means the process of generalization by which ideas connect with other ideas to form more general ideas. As ideas become more general, they incorporate more and more individual events (CP, 1.615). This belief leads to action that produces further beliefs and actions. Concrete reasonableness grows, according to the "law of mind" so that a unity prevails within the individual as well as among individuals.

The unity within the individual develops as the rational ideas "percolate" to the deeper sentiments. At deeper levels the ideas produce the general virtue of self-control, but also such specific virtues as "devotion, courage, loyalty, and modesty" (Sheriff, 87). Of course people can develop these and other virtues without doing philosophy. They learn them through tradition and the instinctual wisdom of human beings. Philosophical reflection and self-criticism enable those who engage in it to become consciously aware of the reasons that certain habits are generally judged as admirable.

But these habits not only integrate the lives of individuals who cultivate them. They also enable such individuals to overcome their self-centeredness and live together in society. The sentiment that leads to moral goodness must be, "a generalized conception of duty which completes [our] personality by melting it into the neighboring part of the universal cosmos" (CP, 1.673). Those who deliberately cultivate the habit of concrete reasonableness as their ultimate aim, not only develop the admirable social and personal virtues, but also consciously strive for concrete reasonableness among individuals. In other words, they work for social unity.

Peirce's statements about unifying society, and individuals melting into neighboring parts of the cosmos, are likely to cause alarms to go off in the minds of many readers. Some might raise the question of whether Peirce's philosophy would naturally lead to a centralization of as many people and resources as possible, for example, the kind implemented by Vladimir Lenin or by Henry Ford. The centralization that took place in government, industry, and technology in the twentieth century, either the Marxian form or the democratic capitalist form, did not resemble Peirce's ideas. A Peircean unity would look very different.

The law of the mind works not by a central power dominating everything beneath it, but by parts being attracted to neighboring parts to form ever more inclusive unities. Peirce made a distinction between power and force. Force is the physical ability to change things, or as Peirce put it, the specialty of force is spoiling things. Power, by contrast, means the exertion of attraction by an ideal. Self-control requires the ability to open ourselves to the attraction of ideals. This ability in turn depends on the ability to be open to that which confronts the self. The confrontation may be with a thought that we perceive as foreign. Reasonableness opposes the natural tendency to see the foreign as an enemy that must be avoided or destroyed. Reasonableness and love enable us to be attracted to ideas and persons who otherwise would be seen as objects to be destroyed lest we be destroyed.

Peirce's notion of agapistic evolution of society, therefore, does not mean a central power collectivizing and thereby stifling individuals. On the contrary it means that individuals continue their own actualization and that of their neighbors by overcoming hostility and uniting in larger communities. The ongoing process never reaches completion for the individual or society. The attraction of reasonableness powers the process, and the process in turn promotes concrete reasonableness. Peirce draws the practical conclusion:

> (Our interests) must not stop at our own fate, but must embrace the whole community....This community, again, must not be limited, but must

extend to all races of being, with whom we can come into immediate or mediate intellectual relation. (CP, 2.654)

Continuity of Practical and Theoretical Ethics

This chapter began with the contention, that contrary to Peirce's disclaimers, we can deem his ethical theory as very valuable for our vital interests. The conclusion does not contradict Peirce, but hopefully clarifies an important aspect of his thought. He contended that practical vital matters and the truths of science must be kept distinct. The kind of ethics needed to solve important vital issues has its best source in instinct and tradition. To attempt to be scientific would hobble a person who needs to make decisions right now. The claim to do this scientifically seems pretentious at best. On the other hand, if ethics takes its place as a branch of philosophy and therefore as a scientific pursuit, it cannot be subservient to any vital interest. Peirce's argument stands.

But over time, even scientific ideas make a difference and serve a purpose for our vital interests. Reason lies on the surface of our soul. The deeper part of the soul, which consists of habits developed by the interaction of instincts and tradition, can better make vital decisions. But the ideas of reason can "percolate" to the deeper regions and influence them. For precisely this reason, ethics must remain free of any kind of self-interest. In order to be beneficial, ideas must be true. That is why Peirce takes the scientist as a paradigm of ethical conduct. The same self criticism that produces right thinking also, when applied to conduct, produces right action. In Peirce's architectonic, logic depends on ethics which in turn depends on esthetics. The science of the *summum bonum*, the admirable in itself, guides the choice of what aims we ought to deliberately choose. The *summum bonum* is the growth of concrete reasonableness. If this idea reaches the deeper part of the soul, we will choose conduct that promotes concrete reasonableness as its deliberately chosen end.

Although this may seem to be an abstract and overly intellectual idea, Peirce reveals it as nothing less than the *agape* which constitutes the principle of evolution and the crowning achievement of the Gospels. Ideas spread and connect with each other and that which was foreign and hateful is made loveable and beautiful and brought into communion. The theoretical ethicist contemplates this idea to the point that it becomes the guiding principle of all thinking, acting, and feeling. Thus, in this slow, indirect, but inexorable manner, the ideals of philosophical ethics touch and affect vital interests.

Conclusion

The study of James, Royce, and Peirce shows, perhaps more clearly than most philosophical studies, that genuine philosophy does not play with abstractions in an idle or dilettantish way. Rather, philosophy constitutes a way of life. As Socrates had shown at the beginning of the philosophical tradition, philosophy is not wisdom but a *way to wisdom*. As William James describes the beams of light that philosophy casts, the worth of philosophy depends on throwing light on our actual lives and giving us a direction and vision to live by.

Three themes permeate each of the three philosophers studied here: the primacy of ethics, the rootedness in science, and the openness to the spiritual aspect of human life. The very name "Pragmatism" implies the primacy of ethics. Thought fulfills its purpose in guiding us to take appropriate action. Ethics studies appropriate action in those areas of life that involves duty and goodness. Unfortunately, popular language often misreads "Pragmatism" to mean expediency without ethics. In this work, I tried to set the record straight and show the intimacy between pragmatism and ethics.

A second theme found in these philosophers shows that pragmatism has deep roots in science. One of the reasons that philosophy has been less effective than it might have been in shaping modern thought results from the perception of philosophy as a weaker and outdated alternative to science. This description is somewhat of a caricature, since many modern philosophers since the time of Descartes had scientific backgrounds and approached problems scientifically. Nevertheless, the caricature remains as the picture held today by many students and educated people outside of philosophy. Another negative view of philosophy sees it tagging along after science and not having much to offer beyond science. The position known as positivism maintains that philosophy in fact has nothing to offer in the way of metaphysics and ethics, and that its role is to serve science by clarifying the language and logic of science. The pragmatists, by contrast, integrated their science with philosophy by not only being intimately knowledgeable of science, but by developing a method that embraces all forms of knowing including science and philosophy. Unlike the positivists, the pragmatists integrated their method with the traditional philosophical problems such as ethics and metaphysics.

The development of ethics and metaphysics opens up the spiritual dimension of life. The positivists tended to be reductionists, reducing ethics to pleasure and pain and dismissing metaphysics. The admiration of science often takes the shape of "scientism," which excludes any nonmeasurable experience from knowledge, and in a more extreme form, contends that what cannot be known scientifically, does not exist. Positivism excluded or dismissed as meaningless such ideas as free will, community, and belief in God. James, Royce, and Peirce, not only showed the reasonableness of believing in such "spiritual" realities, but also showed that they are necessary for a full and good human life

William James placed a priority on ethical action throughout his life. When he was in his late twenties, his cousin Minny Temple, with whom he was very close, died of tuberculosis. He wrote an entry in his diary that expressed his deepest sorrow, but also his lifelong sense of priority. He wrote addressing her:

> By that big part of me that's in the tomb with you, may I realize and believe in the immediacy of death! May I feel that every torment suffered here passes and is a breath of wind—every pleasure too. Acts and examples stay.[1]

Feelings are unimportant compared to action. Like thinking itself, feeling must be subservient to ethical actions. In fact in his theory of emotions James argued that we can best develop a desired emotion by acting as if we already felt the way we desire. Our thoughts and beliefs must also be brought into the service of our actions. This does not mean that we can believe things contrary to facts, or reason. It means that of all the reasonable beliefs consistent with the facts, we may and ought to choose the beliefs most consistent with our ability to act. This assertion explains James's lifelong battle with materialism.

James waged a personal battle against materialism, which he saw as crippling in that it portrays a worldview that excludes free will and the possibility for persons to shape their own destiny. James's pragmatism opens up a view that allows us to believe in real possibilities. He argued for the reasonableness of belief in free will and therefore the belief that we have the opportunity and responsibility to make our world better than it would otherwise be. Reality is infinitely larger than the materialist view can imagine. Contrary to materialism, James's interpretation makes it possible and reasonable to believe in God as the highest power in the universe, who hears our call and shares our deepest hopes. James shows us how to make our life significant and to overcome our blindness toward the joy of other people, and to recognize and fulfill our duty toward the world.

Just as science needs philosophy to prevent it from being too narrow, religion needs philosophy to expand from private experience to pubic discourse. "To redeem religion from unwholesome privacy, and to give public status and universal right of way to its deliverances, has been reason's task" (VRE, 330). Religious feelings and mystical experience provide the source of human knowledge of the divine, but feelings and mysticism cannot be expressed directly in language. By themselves, they would be limited only to those individuals who personally experienced them. But the task of reason, hence of philosophy, is to articulate the meaning of experience so that they may be made accessible to others. Philosophy can guide religion away from exclusiveness and bigotry and thereby enable religion to fulfill its mission of working for universal ideals.

Josiah Royce put so much emphasis on ethical activity that he considered the formation of our very selves to be a duty. Each person has the ethical task of creating and following a plan of life that makes us unique instead of mere members of a species. Royce asserted that the whole of philosophy can be summarized by a single question, "Who am I?" We discover who we are by defining our life plan. In fact, our life plan not only reveals who we are, but also creates who we are.

The individual human becomes a self only by finding and fulfilling his or her unique role in the human community. The community does not stand ready-made, but presents a task for individuals to create. Individual selves cannot exist apart from community and of course, communities cannot exist without individuals. The reciprocal creation of individuals and community constitutes the most fundamental ethical task for human beings. The virtue of loyalty enables us to become good persons in the very act of building community, and thereby loyalty becomes the foundation of all ethics.

Like James, Royce developed a philosophy that enables us to be scientific and religious without falling into a stifling narrowness. In the context of Royce's "far-reaching beams of light" science and religion become expansive. This was made most clear in Royce's *Sources of Religious Insight* as expressed in chapter 10, in which he shows seven stages in the progression of the human self. We move from (1) individual experience, to (2) social experience to (3) reason, from one to many to all. Next came (4) *will*, requiring, us to go beyond experience to action. These four sources provide an indispensable foundation but remain incomplete. The emergence of (5) loyalty directs our action in service to the universal community. The human self must continue to grow through (6) sorrow, by which we get a glimpse of evil assimilated and idealized. Seemingly unrelated meanings are integrated in (7) the unity of the spirit. Royce thereby includes the whole range of human experience in a well-ordered insightful theory.

Finally, we see in **Charles S. Peirce**, the founder of pragmatism, a vision that integrates science, spirituality, and the whole range of human experience, as well as any philosopher ever has. Peirce's misfortune in not being able to secure a position as a university professor may have been an ironic advantage to him as a thinker and therefore to us his readers. He spent much of his productive life as a research scientist and brought the specific skills of the empirical researcher to his grand architectonic of thought. Peirce understood the working of scientific logic practically as well as theoretically. Deductive reasoning enables us to see the implications of any given hypothesis. Inductive reasoning, the work of the experimental scientist, allows us to check the theories against reality. But the marvel of science, what James called "the miracle of miracles" is that the human mind can guess at hypotheses and find that some of them stand up to experimental testing, and therefore are probably true. Peirce saw the same process at work in theoretical ethics, in which we intuit a probable opinion, work out its implications, and test them in terms of our real world.

In Peirce's architectonic, logic is a branch of ethics since logic studies right conduct in the area of thought. Ethics is the study of how to conduct ourselves so as to bring about that which is most admirable. Peirce argues that the most admirable ideal, the province of esthetics, is universal reason. Therefore the scientist, who explicitly works to bring more and more of reality into a rational understanding, stands as the archetype of the ethical person. Peirce saw the fulfillment of the ideal in a movement toward a community that would not be based on conformity or tyranny but would include all persons as autonomous parts of a real community. Peirce believed in God as Creator, but did not see creation as something that was completed "during a busy week in 4004 BC." Creation is still going on and we have our parts to play.

The goal of this present work is to show how the study of each of the three philosophers, James, Royce, and Peirce, provides the basis for a unified vision of contemporary reality in a way that the great ancient and medieval philosopher did for pre-modern times. Whether a person chooses to study one of these philosophers, or takes on the more difficult task of mediating their sometime conflicting views, the study will be as profitable as any philosophical study can be. It will cast what James called the far-reaching beams of light without which we cannot live.

Notes

1. William James, *Pragmatism and the Meaning of Truth* (Cambridge MA: the Harvard University Press, 1978), 10–11; hereafter, *Prag.*

2. A good study of the contrast between classical pragmatism and neo-pragmatism is found in Sandra Rosenthal and Rogene Buchholz, *Rethinking Business Ethics: A Pragmatic Approach* (New York: Oxford University Press, 2000) chap. 4, "Neo-Pragmatism without Pragmatism: A Look at Rorty," 50–65.

3. Joseph Brent, *Charles Sanders Peirce: A Life* (Bloomington, IN: Indiana University Press, 1993), 264; hereafter, Brent.

Part I William James
Chapter 1. Meaning and Truth

1. William James, *Essays in Radical Empiricism and A Pluralistic Universe* (Gloucester, MA: Peter Smith, 1967), 95; hereafter ERE. James first published these essays between 1904 and 1907. He bound them together in a volume and they were published posthumously in 1912. Ralph Barton Perry published them again in 1942 in a single volume with James's 1909 *Pluralistic Universe*; hereafter, PU.

2. In *Pragmatism*, James provides us with an example of a meaningless dispute. A group of campers are in a heated argument. Suppose a hunter sees a squirrel on a tree. The squirrel goes around to the opposite side of the tree and the hunter, keeping his distance walks around the tree. The squirrel continues around to the original side and the hunter continues his path around the tree. If the hunter keeps walking around the tree, and the squirrel keeps the tree between himself and the hunter, *is the hunter walking around the squirrel?* Some of the participants in the debate argue heatedly yes, others heatedly no. James points out that the whole argument is a mere verbal dispute about the phrase "walking around." There is no difference in their understanding of what is happening; pragmatically the views of the two sides are identical.

Chapter 2. Body and Mind

1. Francis Crick, *The Astonishing Hypothesis: The Scientific Search for the Soul* (New York: A Touchstone Book, 1995), 3.

2. Gerald E. Myers, *William James: His Life and Thought* (New Haven, CT: Yale University Press, 1986); hereafter, Myers.

3. Myers observes that James interpreted Berkeley inaccurately. Berkeley affirmed a common world of perception based on God's constant perception (321).

4. Ralph Barton Perry, *The Thought and Character of William James*, 2 vols. (Boston: Little, Brown and Company, 1935), II: 392; hereafter, Perry.

5. As Perry summarized "The Unfinished Task," "'The angel of death' did in fact strike James down before he said all that he had to say. Not only was much left unsaid, but there were many problems that he had neither thought out nor worked out" (Perry II 666–667). Scholars at present have not come to agreement on the meaning and value of radical empiricism. Frank Oppenheim cites Richard Gale's well-supported contention that James dropped the concept of "pure experience" after 1905. Oppenheim observes that, "If Gale interprets James accurately on this point, mainline presentations of James's late thought will require major revisions." (Frank Oppenheim, *Reverence for the Relations of Life*: [Notre Dame, IN: Notre Dame University Press, 2005], 163–164); hereafter, Oppenheim, *Reverence*.

6. William James, *The Will to Believe and Other Essays on Popular Philosophy* (New York: Dover Publications, 1956), 117; hereafter WB.

Chapter 3. Free Will

1. William James, *Principles of Psychology* (New York: Dover Publications, 1950) 2 vols.; hereafter, PP.

2. A. J. Ayer, *The Origins of Pragmatism* (Freeman, Cooper, and Company, 1968), 99.

3. Jean-Paul Sartre, *Being and Nothingness*. (New York: Washington Square Press, 1966), 31.

4. Rollo May, *Love and Will* (New York: Dell Publishing Company, 1969), 220.

5. Alan Watts, "Nature, Man, and Woman," reprinted in *Philosophy Now*, eds. Paula Rothenberg Struhl and Karsten Struhl (New York: Random House, 1975), 499.

Chapter 4. William James and Moral Philosophy

1. William James, *Essays in Faith and Morals*, selected by Ralph Barton Perry (New York: Longmans Green, 1949), 213.

2. Richard Gale gives a magnificent account of this side of James in, "The I-Thou Quest for Intimacy and Religious Mysticism," in *The Divided Self of William James*, chap. 9 (Cambridge, UK: Cambridge University Press, 1999).

Chapter 5. Rationality and Religious Faith

1. William James, *Varieties of Religious Experience* (New York: New American Library, 1958); hereafter VRE.

2. Recent research has shown the physiological basis for these experiences, without discrediting them. *Why God Won't Go Away*, by Andrew Newberg, Eugene D'Aquili, and Vince Raus, is a thorough study of the connection between physiology and spirituality.

3. The reality of intolerance, fanaticism, and religious wars, seems to mock the statement that religion leads to love of neighbor. These hateful reactions occur when the over-beliefs are taken as literal truth and exclusive ways to salvation. *Why God Won't Go Away*, by Andrew Newberg, Eugene D'Aquili, and Vince Rause, gives an interesting explanation of this all too common phenomenon. A person has some taste of the saving power of religion and identifies it exclusively with his or her own tradition taken in a fundamentalist way. It can be summed up by saying a little religion is a dangerous thing. But James's study supports the notion that religion when fully developed and properly understood leads to an attitude of universal love.

4. Linda Simon, *Genuine Reality: A life of William James* (Chicago: The University of Chicago Press, 1998), 199; hereafter, Simon.

5. William James, *Human Immortality: Two Supposed Objection to the Doctrine*, published with *The Will to Believe and Other Essays on Popular Philosophy* (New York: Dover Publications, 1956), 15.

Chapter 6. Human Nature and the Life of the Spirit

1. William James, *The Moral Equivalent of War and Other Essays*, ed. John K. Roth (Harper and Row: Harper Torchbooks), 48.

2. James expressed his struggle to arrive at this conclusion in *A Pluralistic Universe*, especially Lecture V "The Compounding of Consciousness." He had argued in 1890 in *Principles of Psychology* that conscious states could not be made of parts. He affirmed that Berkeley's notion, to be is to be perceived, clearly applies to conscious states. Their whole being consists of being experienced. This reasoning had been at the heart of his rejection of any kind of idealism, including that of Royce, which held that the conscious state of an individual human could also be the conscious state of The Absolute. But, in *A Pluralistic Universe*, James gave a favorable account of the German philosopher, Gustav Fechner, who contended that human consciousness might be part of an earth-soul, which in turn is part of a larger star-soul. Without endorsing the particulars of Fechner, James concluded that the reality of religious experience supports the notion that our consciousness may be part of a higher consciousness. To accept such a view, however, contradicts "The Logic of Identity," which considers a state of consciousness to be this and nothing else. James ultimately

discarded the logic of identity. He argued that the logic that is useful in human life is not adequate for giving us a true knowledge of reality because it makes the universe discontinuous. He summed up his acceptance of the compounding of consciousness at the expense of the logic of identity: "The secret of continuous life which the universe knows by heart and acts on every instant cannot be a contradiction incarnate. If logic says it is one, so much the worse for logic. Logic being the lesser thing, the static incomplete abstraction, must succumb to reality, not reality to logic" (*PU*, 207).

Part II Josiah Royce

Chapter 7. The Idealism of Josiah Royce

1. *The Letters of Josiah Royce*. Edited with an introduction by John Clendenning (Chicago: University of Chicago Press, 1970), introduction, 32.

2. James was also willing to learn from his younger colleague Royce. In his treatment of the psychology of belief he cites Royce's *Religious Aspects of Philosophy* as "...the clearest account of the psychology of belief with which I am acquainted" (*PP* II, 318 fn.). Further, James credited Royce with the "moral insight—consider *every* good as a real good and keep as many as we can" (Oppenheim *Reverence*, 78). As Oppenheim observes, "Royce influenced James more than is commonly acknowledged. For example, well before the appearance of James's *Principles*, Royce was writing James about the stream of consciousness, and the will to believe, about association, attention, recognition, and postulates as well as about the construction and boundaries of consciousness" (76).

3. Josiah Royce, *The World and the Individual*, 2 vols. (Gloucester, MA: Peter Smith, 1976), hereafter, WI.

4. Royce was not convincing on this point. Realist philosophers including Ralph Barton Perry argue that an idea may depend on an object without the object mutually depending on the idea. This controversy, as well as attacks on Royce's system by Dewey and others, is outlined in the context of Royce's life in John Clendenning's *The Life and Thought of Josiah Royce* (Nashville, TN: Vanderbilt University Press, 1999), 267–268.

Chapter 8. Josiah Royce's Concept of the Self

1. One example of the trend toward individualism is the popularity of Ayn Rand. Of course this trend is not universal but it does have important political ramifications.

2. Royce was indebted to William James's discussion of self in James's *Principles of Psychology*.

3. Royce is not referring to conformity to, or to rebellion against, finite authority. A person may rebel against an injustice in the name of a higher loyalty such as

individual freedom and dignity. This will become clear in the following chapter on loyalty and ethics.

Chapter 9. Josiah Royce's Philosophy of Loyalty as the Basis for Ethics

1. Josiah Royce, *The Philosophy of Loyalty* (Nashville, TN: Vanderbilt University Press, 1995); hereafter, PL.

2. Frank M Oppenheim, *Royce's Mature Ethics* (Notre Dame, IN: University of Notre Dame Press, 1993), 1–22; hereafter, Oppenheim, *Ethics*.

3. Richard P. Mullin, "Josiah Royce's Philosophy of Loyalty as a Basis for Democratic Ethics," in *Democracy and the Post-Totalitarian Experience* (Value Inquiry Book Series volume 167. New York: Rodopi NY, 2005), 183–191. The material on loyalty is essentially from my Value Inquiry Book contribution with some changes due to context. I gratefully acknowledge Rodopi's permission policy.

4. Oppenheim, *Ethics*. Appendix C. For any correct insight in this chapter I am indebted to this work of Frank Oppenheim.

5. Josiah Royce, *Studies of Good and Evil: A Series of Essays Upon the Problems of Philosophy and Life* (Hamden CT: Archon Books, 1964); hereafter SGE.

6. Josiah Royce, *The Problem of Christianity* (Washington, DC The Catholic University of America Press, 2001); hereafter, PC.

Chapter 10. The Religious Insights of Josiah Royce

1. Josiah Royce, *The Sources of Religious Insight* (New York: Charles Scribners Sons, 1912); hereafter, SRI.

2. Scott Peck, in *A Different Drum*, describes the awareness of chaos and need for order to show how some people can be good soldiers but cannot handle the lack of structure in civilian life, or model prisoners but cannot stay free of crime when they are released.

3. I found this quote from Perry in Ellen Kappy Suckiel's *Heavens Champion: William James's Philosophy of Religion*. (Notre Dame, IN: Notre Dame Press. 1996), 41.

Part III Charles Sanders Peirce
Chapter 11. Peirce and the Origin of Pragmatism

1. Kenneth Laine Kettner, *His Glassy Essence: An Autobiography of Charles Sanders Peirce* (Nashville, TN: Vanderbilt University Press, 1998), 39.

2. Brent. On pages 7–9 of his *Life*, Brent gives a very succinct account of Peirce's obscurity at the time of his death and of the efforts that have led to the recent recognition of his importance. The work of making Peirce's writings more accessible continues under the leadership of Nathan Houser, director of the Peirce Edition Project at Indiana University—Purdue University at Indianapolis.

3. The biographical studies of Pierce include Kenneth Laine Kettner's, *His Glassy Essence: An Autobiography of Charles Sanders Peirce*. The author takes on the voice of a detective mystery writer who happens on a manuscript of Peirce's proposed but unfinished autobiography. The work is constructed from Peirce's letters and other first person statements. Other biographical accounts include Joseph *Brent's Charles Sanders Peirce: A Life*; Louis Menand's, *The Metaphysical Club* (New York: Farrar, Straus and Giroux, 2001); hereafter Menand. Menand's book is a very readable and exciting narrative not only of Peirce, but of several of his contemporaries and fellow giants of American thought.

4. Charles Sanders Peirce, *Collected Papers,* vols. I–VI, ed. Charles Hartshorne and Paul Weiss, 1931–1935; vols. VII-VIII, ed. A. Burks, 1958) CP, 5.388–410; hereafter, CP with volume and paragraph numbers.

5. Meaninglessness is illustrated by James example in endnote 2.

6. The following description of Peirce's development is based on Menand, 221–230; and Karl-Otto Apel, *Charles S. Peirce: From Pragmatism to Pragmaticism* (New Jersy: Humanities Press, 1981) 56–60; hereafter Otto-Apel.

7. Karl-Otto Apel, Charles S. Peirce, 57.

Chapter 12. Charles Sanders Peirce on the Human Person

1. Peirce's travails are described by Joseph Brent and Kenneth Kettner. For example, Peirce was denied his dream of an academic career in spite of his obvious brilliance, his family connections as the son of a distinguished Harvard professor, and the strong support of William James and Josiah Royce.

2. Vincent Colapietro presents a developmental interpretation of Peirce's theory of the person in "Peirce's Account of the Self: A Developmental Perspective," *Peirce's Approach to the Self: A Semiotic Approach to Human Subjectivity*, chap. 4 Albany: State University of New York Press, 1989; hereafter, Colapietro. The exposition given here is not an attempt to present Colapietro's account, but it is highly dependent on it. My brief chapter on Peirce's view of the self brings nothing new to the table, but is a necessary piece of information for the context of the following chapter on ethics.

Chapter 13. Ethics and the Purpose of Human Life

1. Vincent G. Potter S. J. points out that when Peirce wrote his observation on the popularity of Darwinism, Lamarckism was considered to be a viable scientific

alternative. *Charles S. Peirce on Norms and Ideals* (Worcester, MA: The University of Massachusetts Press, 1967), 177. As Potter points out, the question at hand is not whether further evidence would support Darwin, but rather, why Darwin was so enthusiastically accepted before the evidence was in.

2. An example of relativist virtue ethics shows up in Robert Solomon's *Ethics and Excellence: Cooperation and Integrity in Business* (New York: Oxford University Press, 1993). Solomon models his ethics after Aristotle but cautions: "Philosophers have often argued that morality is defined in part by its universality, but few ethicists have been tempted to say that about virtues. Indeed, the most striking thing about virtues is how they vary from culture to culture and throughout history" (196). Solomon provides an excellent example of practical ethics, and Peirce would presumably applaud him for avoiding claims of universal scientific validity. But Solomon does not advocate complete relativism. He responds to the charge that his community-based virtue ethics could not declare slavery or oppression wrong if it is condoned by a particular community: "My answer is that, without being romantic or utopian, there is such a thing as the human community, and there are certain foundations to our behavior in what is called 'human nature'" (206). If we may speak of a "Peircean" virtue ethics, it is also community-based, but the community is the evolving universal society.

3. Karl-Otto Apel connects Peirce's Pragmatic method for clarifying ideas to his highest ethical norm and to the formation of habits, or virtues. After explaining that Peirce's reasoning on the highest goals of our action goes beyond the framework of pragmatism in the narrow technical sense he observes: "Nonetheless, Peirce does not give up the principle of clarifying thought by means of attention to practical consequences. This is because the 'manner' in which he serves the *summum bonum* by furthering 'concrete reasonableness' does not have the character of an abstract general concept.... Rather it has the form of a rule embedded in human behavior, and for Peirce its character is that of a real universal.... We are concerned here with a habit in which the universal concept must be incarnated, in a way, as a rule for possible human behavior if a man is not only to understand the meaning of a statement, but also to believe that this statement is binding for him" (Apel, 89).

4. John K. Sheriff, *Peirce's Guess at the Riddle: Grounds for Human Significance* (Bloomington and Indianapolis, IN: Indiana University Press, 1994), 68–69; hereafter, Sheriff.

Conclusion

1. Gay Wilson Allen, *William James: A Biography* (New York: The Viking Press, 1967), 167.

Bibliography

Allen, Gay Wilson. *William James: A Biography.* New York: The Viking Press, 1967.

Apel, Karl-Otto. *Charles S. Peirce: From Pragmatism to Pragmaticism.* New Jersey: Humanities Press, 1981.

Ayers, A. J. *The Origins of Pragmatism.*: Freeman, Cooper, and Company, 1968.

Brent, Joseph. *Charles Sanders Peirce: A Life.* Bloomington, IN: Indiana University Press, 1993.

Clendenning, John. *The Life and Thought of Josiah Royce.* Nashville, TN: Vanderbilt University Press, 1999.

Colapietro, Vincent. *Peirce's Approach to the Self: A Semiotic Approach to Human Subjectivity.* Albany: State University of New York Press, 1989.

Crick, Francis. *The Astonishing Hypothesis: The Scientific Search for the Soul.* New York: A Touchstone Book, 1995.

Gale, Richard. *The Divided Self of William James.* Cambridge UK: Cambridge University Press, 1999.

James, William. *Essays in Faith and Morals.* Selected by Ralph Barton Perry. New York: Longmans Green, 1949.

———. *Essays in Radical Empiricism and A Pluralistic Universe.* Gloucester, MA: Peter Smith, 1967.

———. *Human Immortality: Two Supposed Objection to the Doctrine.* Published with *The Will to Believe and Other Essays on Popular Philosophy.* New York: Dover Publications, 1956.

———. *The Moral Equivalent of War and Other Essays.* Edited by John K. Roth.: Harper and Row: Harper Torchbooks.

———. *Pragmatism and the Meaning of Truth.* Cambridge, MA: Harvard University Press, 1978.

———. *Principles of Psychology.* New York: Dover Publications, 1950.

———. *Varieties of Religious Experience.* New York: New American Library, 1958.

———. *The Will to Believe and Other Essays on Popular Philosophy.* New York: Dover Publications, 1956.

Kettner, Kenneth Laine. *His Glassy Essence: An Autobiography of Charles Sanders Peirce.* Nashville, IN: Vanderbilt University Press, 1998.

May, Rollo. *Love and Will.* New York: Dell Publishing Company, 1969.

Menand, Louis. *The Metaphysical Club.* New York: Farrar, Straus and Giroux, 2001.

Mullin, Richard P. "Josiah Royce's Philosophy of Loyalty As a Basis for Democratic Ethics." in *Democracy and the Post-Totalitarian Experience.* Value Inquiry Book Series Volume 167. New York: Rodopi, NY, 2005.

Myers, Gerald E. *William James: His Life and Thought.* New Haven, CT: Yale University Press, 1986.

Newberg, Andrew, Eugene D'Aquili, and Vince Rause. *Why God Won't go Away.* New York: Balantine Books, 2002.

Oppenheim, Frank M. *Reverence for the Relations of Life: Re-imagining Pragmatism via Josiah Royce's Interactions with Peirce, James, and Dewey.* Notre Dame, IN: University of Notre Dame Press, 2005.

———. *Royce's Mature Ethics.* Notre Dame, IN: University of Notre Dame Press, 1993.

Peirce, Charles Sanders. *Collected Papers.* Cambridge: Harvard University Press. Electronic Version, InteLex Corporation.

Perry, Ralph Barton. *The Thought and Character of William James.* Boston: Little, Brown and Company, 1935.

Potter, Vincent. *Charles S. Peirce on Norms and Ideals.* Amherst, MA: University of Massachusetts Press, 1967.

Rosenthal, Sandra B., and Rogene Buchholz. *Rethinking Business Ethics: A Pragmatic Approach.* New York: Oxford University Press, 2000.

Royce, Josiah. *The Letters of Josiah Royce.* Edited with an introduction by John Clendenning. Chicago: University of Chicago Press, 1970.

————. *Metaphysics*. Edited by Richard Hocking and Frank Oppenheim. Albany: New York University Press, 1998.

————. *The Philosophy of Loyalty*. Nashville, TN: Vanderbilt University Press, 1995.

————. *The Problem of Christianity*. Washington, DC: The Catholic University of America Press, 2001.

————. *The Sources of Religious Insight*. New York: Charles Scribners Sons, 1912.

————. *Studies of Good and Evil: A Series of Essays upon the Problems of Philosophy and Life*. Hamden, CT: Archon Books, 1964.

————. *The World and the Individual*. 2 vols. Gloucester, MA: Peter Smith, 1976.

Sartre, Jean-Paul. *Being and Nothingness*. New York: Washington Square Press, 1966.

Sheriff, John K. *Peirce's Guess at the Riddle: Grounds for Human Significance*. Bloomington and Indianapolis, IN: Indiana University Press, 1994.

Simon, Linda. *Genuine Reality: A Life of William James*. Chicago: The University of Chicago Press, 1998.

Suckiel, Ellen Kappy. Heavens *Champion: William James's Philosophy of Religion*. Notre Dame, IN: University of Notre Dame Press, 1996.

Watts, Alan. "Nature, Man, and Woman." Reprinted in *Philosophy Now*. Edited by Paula Rothenberg Struhl and Karsten Struhl. New York: Random House, 1975.

Index